Palgrave Studies in Victims and Victimology

Series Editors
Matthew Hall
University of Lincoln
Lincoln, UK

Pamela Davies
Department of Social Sciences
Northumbria University
Newcastle upon Tyne, UK

In recent decades, a growing emphasis on meeting the needs and rights of victims of crime in criminal justice policy and practice has fuelled the development of research, theory, policy and practice outcomes stretching across the globe. This growth of interest in the victim of crime has seen victimology move from being a distinct subset of criminology in academia to a specialist area of study and research in its own right.

Palgrave Studies in Victims and Victimology showcases the work of contemporary scholars of victimological research and publishes some of the highest-quality research in the field. The series reflects the range and depth of research and scholarship in this burgeoning area, combining contributions from both established scholars who have helped to shape the field and more recent entrants. It also reflects both the global nature of many of the issues surrounding justice for victims of crime and social harm and the international span of scholarship researching and writing about them.

More information about this series at
http://www.palgrave.com/gp/series/14571

Catherine Donovan • Rebecca Barnes

Queering Narratives of Domestic Violence and Abuse

Victims and/or Perpetrators?

palgrave
macmillan

Catherine Donovan
Durham University
Durham, UK

Rebecca Barnes
University of Leicester
Leicester, UK

Palgrave Studies in Victims and Victimology
ISBN 978-3-030-35402-2   ISBN 978-3-030-35403-9   (eBook)
https://doi.org/10.1007/978-3-030-35403-9

Cover illustration: Morna Simpson

This Palgrave Pivot imprint is published by the registered company Springer Nature Switzerland AG.
The registered company address is: Gewerbestrasse 11, 6330 Cham, Switzerland

Acknowledgements

Catherine and Rebecca acknowledge the following, without whom the Coral Project would not have happened: the Economic and Social Research Council for funding the Coral Project (research grant number ES/J0125801/); our steering group with members from Respect, The Scottish Transgender Alliance, Safer Wales, NEDAP, Broken Rainbow, LGBT Youth Scotland, National Offender Management Service (now HMPPS), and Professor Nicole Westmarland from Durham University; the research team which included Dr Catherine Nixon and Paula Willerton; the over 200 organisations who agreed to circulate our recruitment literature for the survey amongst their networks; and the many organisations and individuals who helped us recruit and host focus groups and interviews with practitioners. We also thank each and every practitioner who agreed to take part in either focus groups or interviews.

Both Durham University and the University of Leicester provided further financial support to us to be able to pay for editorial assistance and employ Dr Sarah Hodgkinson to provide statistical assistance. Thanks also to Joseph White for producing the Coral Project Power, Control and Space for Reaction Wheel. We give special thanks to Melissa Girling for the unstinting work she did on the bibliographies for each chapter.

We thank Palgrave Macmillan, especially Liam Inscoe-Jones, for their efficiency and support during this book project.

Catherine also thanks Melissa for her love and support throughout the writing of this book. Rebecca thanks Morna for her love, support and patience during the writing of this book, and her colleagues in the School of Criminology at the University of Leicester for their support and encouragement.

Last, but not least, our special thanks go to every LGB and/or T+ person who took part in the survey, especially those who agreed to take part in the follow-up interviews. Your openness and willingness to talk about your experiences of being victimised as well as of using violence and 'abusive' behaviours have been inspirational to us. We dedicate this book to you.

Praise for *Queering Narratives of Domestic Violence and Abuse*

"Drawing on an innovative methodology, Donovan and Barnes make an important contribution to the field with a discussion of relevance to practitioners, policymakers and researchers alike, critiquing assumptions and binaries that have real world consequences, not least the misapplied label of 'mutual abuse'. The significance of this book is that Donovan and Barnes both advance the LGB and T literature while challenging us all to rethink some of the assumptions that underpin the wider domestic abuse field."

—James Rowlands, *LGBT domestic abuse campaigner and independent consultant, and former commissioner*

Contents

About the Authors

Catherine Donovan is Professor of Sociology at Durham University. She has been researching the intimate and family lives of LGB and, more recently, T+ people for over 30 years. Most recently, she has been focussing on experiences and uses of intimate partner violence and abuse. Other work includes on hate crime, particularly on hate relationships, and campus safety.

Rebecca Barnes has been researching and teaching about domestic violence and abuse for more than 15 years, focussing especially on LGB and/ or T+ people's relationships, and more recently on domestic abuse and the church. She is Senior Research Adviser in Qualitative and Social Research Methods for the NIHR Research Design Service East Midlands, based at the University of Leicester.

List of Tables

1

Introduction

Abstract Chapter 1 sets out the central concerns of this book and introduces the key conceptual tools on which our sociological analysis draws. We briefly review existing research on intimate partner violence and abuse (IPVA) in LGB and/or T+ people's relationships and explain why we do not dismiss feminist theorising in making sense of this. Our central argument, informed by Michael Johnson's typology, is that there are different kinds of IPVA and that it is essential in research and practice to distinguish between them. We unpack how the impact of the public story of domestic violence and abuse means that IPVA in LGB and/or T+ people's relationships is often perceived to be mutual abuse. We extend this public story to include how a binary of ideal victim/perpetrator inhibits those who are being victimised and who enact what we call 'space for reaction'—the range of violent and non-violent behaviours which victimised partners might use in response to coercively controlling partners— from recognising their victimisation. We outline how our analysis is both intersectional and ecological, accounting for not only the multiple identities inhabited by participants, but also the wider social and cultural context through which structural inequalities are reproduced.

© The Author(s) 2020
C. Donovan, R. Barnes, *Queering Narratives of Domestic Violence and Abuse*, Palgrave Studies in Victims and Victimology, https://doi.org/10.1007/978-3-030-35403-9_1

Keywords Cisnormativity • Coercive control • Domestic violence and abuse • Ecological analysis • Feminist theory • Heteronormativity • Intimate partner violence and abuse • Lesbian, gay, bisexual and/or transgender • Intersectionality • Minority stress • Mutual abuse • Perpetrators • Public story of domestic violence and abuse • Typologies of domestic violence and abuse

1.1   Introduction

This book explores the use of physical violence and other behaviours that could be perceived to be abusive in the relationships of lesbians, gay men, bisexual women and men, and/or transgender women and men and non-binary gender and/or genderqueer people (LGB and/or T+). The Coral Project is a mixed-methods research project carried out in the United Kingdom (UK) to find out 'what you do when things go wrong in your relationship', involving a national community survey of LGB and/or T+ people and follow-up interviews with volunteers from the survey. Interviews also took place with providers of both mandatory and voluntary perpetrator interventions for heterosexual, ostensibly cisgender men, and focus groups with a range of practitioner groups providing what we broadly call 'relationships services' (Donovan et al. 2014). This book focusses on key findings from the survey and interviews with LGB and/or T+ participants. We believe that our work is a reminder about the instability of research about intimate partner violence and abuse (IPVA) that relies on a narrow incident- or act-based approach, rather than research that attempts to provide a more holistic exploration of the relationships within which IPVA occurs. We are concerned with the different stories that can be told about IPVA depending on the data collected and the analysis undertaken.

Before we outline the structure and key themes of the book, a note about terminology is required. Whilst we use the term LGB and/or T+ to include the diversity of sexuality and gender identities that exist and to recognise that not all trans+ people identify as LGB, when discussing other authors' work we use their chosen terminology, such as 'same-sex relationships'. The phrase 'violence and other behaviours that could be perceived to be abusive' indicates our view that context, meanings, motives and impacts are crucial to making sense of these behaviours in an intimate relationship. Having made this point, and for brevity, throughout the rest of the book we sometimes refer to violence and 'abusive' behaviours, placing 'abusive' in scare quotes to remind the reader that the judgement of whether the behaviours are abusive is contingent. We use the acronym IPVA to refer to all violent and 'abusive' behaviours that might be experienced or enacted in adult intimate relationships. Throughout this book we also refer to domestic violence and abuse (DVA) as the most impactful and serious form of IPVA: what Johnson (2008) would call coercively controlling violence (CCV) and Stark (2007) coercive control. We use this term because it is the most often used in the UK context and because it aligns with the England and Wales Home Office definition (Home Office 2013). However, whilst the Home Office definition includes an incident-based approach to defining DVA, we focus on that part of the definition that depicts a 'pattern of incidents of controlling, coercive or threatening behaviour, violence or abuse' (Home Office 2013, p. 2) and restrict our concern to adult intimate relationships.

A core argument underpinning this book is that safe and best practice responses are best informed by recognising that there are different kinds of IPVA. Below, we outline the typology of IPVA that we have used as the basis of our analysis. The field of IPVA has been dominated by a focus on the IPVA perpetrated by ostensibly heterosexual, cisgender men against ostensibly heterosexual, cisgender women. By cisgender we mean individuals whose gender identity aligns with the sex to which they were assigned at birth. We say 'ostensibly' because, typically, in the mainstream research on IPVA, neither the gender identity nor indeed even the sexuality of either the person reporting victimisation or their partner is asked about (e.g. Walby et al. 2017); thus assumptions are made that data refers to heterosexual IPVA (Donovan and Barnes 2019). This book therefore queers mainstream research about IPVA by exposing its widespread heteronormativity and cisnormativity and by being clear about when participants' sexuality and/or gender identity are known or assumed.

Hereafter, we use 'HC women' to mean heterosexual, cisgender women and 'HC men' to refer to heterosexual, cisgender men.

1.2   Key Concerns of This Book

Two major concerns run through this book: how knowledge and explanatory frameworks about IPVA are produced. There are obvious overlaps in that methodological approaches are informed by researchers' disciplinary origins, which provide particular epistemological and ontological approaches towards meaning-making and knowledge production about the world. Arguably, the production of knowledge about IPVA has developed as the case for a more sociological and holistic approach to understanding IPVA has been successfully made. Indeed, a pioneer of research about IPVA in lesbian relationships, Janice Ristock, evidenced the different ways in which IPVA might be enacted in her Canadian qualitative research before the idea of typologies of violence had really taken hold in the mainstream field. Her post-structuralist feminist analysis led her to critique the binaries of perpetrator/victim, male/female as irrelevant for her participants, whose accounts demonstrated how individuals might be both perpetrators and victims in the same and/or across different relationships, and that violence might be motivated for many reasons, including to control, defend, retaliate, for revenge. In a 'refusal of the social science/social service drive to create all-explanatory models', she resisted any attempt to theorise a 'new model for understanding lesbian relationship violence' (Ristock 2002, p. xi). Rather, she insisted that each case should be taken as an individual relationship experience that should not be expected to fit a pattern. We similarly resist any attempts to apply heteronormative, cisnormative theorising uncritically to the experiences of LGB and/or T+ people; however, we do intend to explore the ways in which a typology might provide a basis for operationalising the knowledge Ristock produced about the limitations of existing binaries.

In the mainstream, cisnormative, heteronormative IPVA field, quantitative methodologies have expanded from simply counting violent and/or 'abusive' acts (prevalence) and their frequencies (incidence). Identifying behavioural or social factors in the partner who has been victimised and/

or the violent or 'abusive' partner that correlate with their victimisation or perpetration, measuring the impacts of those acts, including a wider range of acts, and exploring the motives behind those acts (Hamby 2009) are now also considered. However, we would still argue that these methodologies are limited by a presumption in the survey design of IPVA as being constructed through incidents and essentialised categories of victim and perpetrator.

Our second concern is the explanatory frameworks that exist for IPVA, which both derive from and underpin the methodological approaches taken to produce knowledge about IPVA. Whilst this book is focussed on IPVA in the relationships of LGB and/or T+ people, our theoretical and methodological journeys originate in feminist analyses of violence against HC women. Theorising about IPVA typically comes from sociological or psychological disciplinary origins, including attempts to combine the two (e.g. Heise 1998). Feminist-informed theorising typically foregrounds sociological explanations (Johnson and Ferraro 2000), problematising gender (Johnson et al. 2014), gender orders and regimes (Walby 1990; Wilcox 2006), family, intimacy and power (Dobash and Dobash 1979). In other words, feminist sociological approaches explore the relationship contexts within which IPVA occurs, rather than only focussing on the incidents. We endeavour to bring this lens to IPVA in the relationships of LGB and/or T+ people.

1.3   Researching IPVA in the Relationships of LGB and/or T+ People: Stories of Invisibility

Whilst research on IPVA in the relationships of LGB and/or T+ people has increased, it remains marginal in the field of IPVA, and only recently have large random population samples started to make LGB respondents visible (see Donovan and Hester 2014; Messinger 2017 for overviews). This is a promising development as it opens up the possibilities of collecting more robust data (albeit only about victimisation, to date). However, often general population surveys tell a frustratingly partial story due to heteronormative, cisnormative assumptions being made about respondents' sexuality and gender identity, while typically the gender and/or sexuality of their partner(s) are not captured (see also Duke and Davidson 2009; Head and Milton 2014). For example, recently the Office for National Statistics (ONS) analysed figures on 'partner abuse' from the Crime Survey for England and Wales (CSEW). They focussed only on the women participants (cisgender identity is assumed in the survey) and analysed their responses by sexuality. Bisexual women (10.9%) and lesbians (8%) were more likely to report partner abuse than HC women (6%) (ONS 2018; mirroring Walters et al. 2013 in the USA). Not knowing the gender or sexuality of the partners who perpetrated partner abuse leaves us having to speculate about the disproportionately higher rates of partner abuse amongst LB women. It is possible that many of the perpetrators are HC men (see Ristock 2011 and Donovan and Hester 2014 for similar speculations about other, similar research). The age of the sample might also be implicated since younger people are both more likely to report IPVA (ONS 2018) and to identify as bisexual (ONS 2015).

Turning to research targeting LGB and/or T+ people, most of this has either focussed on lesbians and gay men or in other ways defined its intended target sample as people in 'same-sex' relationships, regardless of the sexuality and/or gender identity of the participants. A similar lack of attention to the sexuality and/or gender identity of the partner being reported on is found in this research (see Edwards et al. 2015). Any particularities of experience for bisexual people are rarely made visible (Head and Milton 2014). Similarly, trans+ people are rarely visible in research on IPVA; however, emerging studies indicate even higher rates of victimisation than among cisgender LGB people (Bachman and Gooch 2018; Guadalupe-Diaz and Jasinski 2017; Messinger 2017).

Similar methodological problems exist in research on IPVA in the relationships of LGB and/or T+ people as in the mainstream. Systematic reviews of the literature on IPVA in same-sex relationships (Kimmes et al. 2019), IPVA between men who have sex with men (Finneran and Stephenson 2012), psychological aggression in LGB intimate relationships (Mason et al. 2014) and IPVA amongst LGB populations (Edwards et al. 2015) all highlight inconsistencies in the definitions of violence and abuse used, the recall periods and the types of violence focussed on, as well as issues with representativeness. We return to these issues in Chap. 2.

Whilst surveys on IPVA victimisation are increasing, research on perpetration is under-developed in the relationships of LGB and/or T+ people (see Finneran and Stephenson 2012). Mason et al. (2014) found psychological aggression perpetration rates of between 6% and 96.4% in studies of cisgender gay and bisexual men, and of between 16.3% and 97.6% among cisgender lesbian and bisexual women. In their review of IPVA, Edwards et al. (2015) found a range from 1% of forced sex perpetration among current relationships of LGBT individuals to 97% perpetration of a combined measure of psychological, sexual and physical violence in a survey of LGB individuals. The authors acknowledge that such a range of rates and measures used, often with self-selecting samples, sheds little light on the prevalence of perpetration or victimisation of IPVA (Edwards et al. 2015). Nevertheless, these studies establish the visibility of the problem of IPVA in the relationships of LGB and/or T+ people and evidence the need for better methodologies for explicating it. Apart from prevalence studies, there has also been an increase in quantitative correlational research.

1.4 Correlating Factors with Perpetration of IPVA

Increasingly, researchers of IPVA in the relationships of LGB and/or T+ people are rejecting feminist theorising and gender as a central explanatory concept, in favour of more psycho-social accounts of the impacts of minority stress on IPVA victimisation and perpetration (Balsam and Szymanski 2005; Finneran and Stephenson 2012; Kimmes et al. 2019; Mendoza 2011). In this literature, individuals' inability to psychologically adapt either to their own sexuality and/or transgender identity (through coming or being out) or the stress of living with homo/bi/transphobia is identified as the reason why they become victims or perpetrators of IPVA. We agree that living in a world that has historically pathologised, morally problematised and criminalised those who are

LGB and/or T+ can have profoundly negative impacts on LGB and/or T+ people's expectations about their possibilities for living happy intimate and family lives (Donovan and Barnes 2018). Indeed, throughout this book we critique how the mainstream field of IPVA has produced a heteronormative, cisnormative public story of DVA (see below) that has profound impacts on recognition and help-seeking amongst LGB and/or T+ people (Donovan and Barnes in press; Donovan and Hester 2014).

However, we disagree that decisions about being out and experiences of homo/bi/transphobia always result in poor mental health. Rather, decisions about being out can be rational, arrived at through assessments of safety, support, honesty and/or empowerment (Seidman et al. 1999), while impacts of homo/bi/transphobia might also include empowerment (Donovan et al. 2018) and anger as well as fear. We also question the utility of correlations between various markers for minority stress and either victimisation or perpetration when the logic of the argument seems flawed (Donovan 2015; Donovan and Hester 2014). If we applied the same logic to other minoritised groups such as HC women, we might expect to see far more HC men being victimised by HC women who have experienced misogyny, and far more white people being victimised by Black people who have experienced racism, yet this is not evident. Finally, our sociological lens leads us away from individual responsibility or pathology to considering the role of society in creating the conditions in which IPVA can occur and what might be done to ameliorate those conditions for LGB and/or T+ people.

Besides this emphasis on minority stress, a second strand of correlation research examines predictive and/or co-existing social and/or behavioural factors that have also been linked to IPVA perpetration by, typically, HC men. Messinger (2017) identifies the factors as socialisation, power imbalances, dependency, justifications, psychological traits and gender (see also Edwards et al. 2015). The same factors are asked about and identified as important regardless of the sample population being studied. For example, Wu et al.'s (2014) study of Black men who have sex with men finds significant correlations between substance use and IPVA victimisation and perpetration, previous child abuse, or family violence. Toro-Alfonso and Rodriguez-Madera (2004) also talk about childhood history and substance use being correlated with the use of IPVA in the Puerto

Rican gay male couples in their study. However, a limitation of these studies is that they typically count as a perpetrator anybody who reports enacting any violent act, regardless of their motives or the relationship context (e.g. Bartholomew et al. 2008; Carvalho et al. 2011). The slippage that often occurs between correlation and causation is another reason for caution.

1.5   The Relevance of Feminist Theory

The development of alternative theoretical explanatory frameworks for IPVA in the relationships of LGB and/or T+ people seems to derive from arguments about the apparent irrelevance of feminist theory in these contexts. First of all, we cannot agree that there is an absence of 'gender relations' (see Frankland and Brown 2014), or patriarchy (see Cannon and Buttell 2015) in 'same-sex' relationships because of the absence of an HC man. These arguments imply that at the moment they come out and/or transition and/or enter a relationship, LGB and/or T+ people enter a separate social world uninfluenced by the heteronormatively, cisnormatively gendered world they have hitherto inhabited (see also Baker et al. 2013). Stark (2007, 2010) has argued that coercively controlling behaviour operates through a patriarchal set of expectations about HC women's gender role held by HC men that are reinforced societally (Stark 2007). The cumulative impact is 'micro-regulation' of the HC woman's life by her HC male partner, experienced as entrapment. In his most recent work with Hester, Stark recognises that it is not only 'sexual inequality' but also 'heteronormativity' that will 'shape abuse in all relational settings' (Stark and Hester 2019, p. 92), but the authors also argue that the knowledge base is insufficient to explicate coercive control in 'LGBT relationships'. Johnson has more recently recognised that CCV can take place within any kind of relationship, regardless of sexuality or gender (Johnson et al. 2014). However, he argues that the evidence points to (HC) men in relationships with (HC) women being the predominant perpetrators of CCV.

Yet, qualitative research about IPVA in the relationships of LGB and/or T+ people's relationships suggests otherwise. It is always important to take account of the national and cultural context in which studies of IPVA are undertaken, yet there is evidence that an association between heteronormative, cisnormative masculinity and IPVA is common across different samples of gay men. In their study of 117 cisgender, mostly gay men in the USA who were from diverse national, ethnic and racial origins, Oringher and Samuelson (2011, p. 72) found that conformity to what they called a 'traditional' masculinity, that is, aggression and inability to show emotional vulnerability, was much more likely to be correlated with physical violence perpetration rather than victimisation. Another study in the USA (Goldenberg et al. 2016) used focus groups to explore with a group of cisgender, mostly gay and some bisexual men who were majority African American (53%) and Caucasian white (47%), whether they felt the violence and abuse items in a common IPVA measurement tool, the CTS2 (discussed in Chap. 2), were relevant to IPVA in gay male relationships and what other behaviours might be relevant. Whilst participants were not asked about personal experiences of IPVA, many drew on first- or second-hand experiences. Many of the participants expected men to want to establish their 'alpha' position in their intimate relationship, underlining the adoption of the heteronormative male/female binary as a template for an unequal intimacy.

Traditional norms of gender have also been implicated in the way that African American lesbians might be perceived by the police or other help providers. Hill et al. (2012, p. 409) discuss the way in which African American women are 'are already seen as innately aggressive and masculinized' and that this might act as a barrier to being recognised as the victimised partner and/or or being in need of any help, either because of her perceived strength or her responsibility for her situation. Hassouneh and Glass (2008) found similar findings in their qualitative study with 57 women, including a transgender woman, of whom seven identified as a perpetrator of violence against a female same-sex partner. Assumptions about heteronormative cisnormative gender roles are described by participants as being relied on by the police in making decisions: perpetrators played on these assumptions by performing a 'feminine victim role' (Hassouneh and Glass 2008, p. 321) in front of the police in order to deflect attention away from their perpetration, while victimised partners who were deemed more masculine than their abusive partner were arrested and/or not believed (Hassouneh and Glass 2008; see also Donovan and Hester 2014). Similarly, in Brown's (2011) qualitative study of women who had experienced IPVA in relationships with transgender men, beliefs about cisgender masculinity and male roles underpinned some of their experiences. These studies all support our argument that the relationships of LGB and/or T+ people are shaped by patriarchal ideas about heteronormative, cisnormative femininity and masculinity that have consequences both within relationships and with regard to the perceptions of those external to them.

This book builds on the work of Donovan and Hester (2014), who provide three core ideas that follow from a feminist analysis recognising the impact of patriarchal, heteronormative, cisnormative ideas on meaning-making about IPVA in the relationships of LGB and/or T+ people: the public story of DVA, the relationship rules in DVA relationships and the impacts of practices of love, all discussed next.

1.5.1 Developing the Public Story of DVA

Donovan and Hester (2010, 2014) argue that, notwithstanding the success of feminist scholarship and activism in transforming DVA from a private trouble to a public problem (Mills 1959), there has been an unintended consequence. The production of a dominant public story (Jamieson 1998) about DVA constructs it as a problem of heterosexual, and we would say, cisgender, men for HC women; a problem predominantly of physical violence, which we would say reinforces the story that IPVA is about incidents of violence; and a problem of a particular presentation of gender: a big, 'strong', HC man being physically violent towards a small, 'weak', HC woman. This public story acts as a barrier to recognising DVA, both for LGB and/or T+ people themselves and for help providers (Donovan and Hester 2010, 2014). In this story, only HC women can be victimised, and only HC men can be perpetrators. In a relationship between two women or two men, any violence must be equal, because they are assumed to be equally matched; and the violence will not be very serious, either because they are women and women are not violent, or because they are men and used to fighting and defending themselves (Duke and Davidson 2009).

Consequently, any IPVA enacted between two self-identified women or men can be read as an equal fight, or not as serious or risky as that portrayed in the public story DVA enacted by an HC man towards an HC woman (Renzetti 1992). Several comparative studies with different practitioners, such as the police, refuge workers, psychology students and potential jury members, have shown how assumptions about risk, safety and escalation have been shaped by the public story of DVA, resulting in violence between two women or two men being seen as less risky, less likely to escalate, less needing of police intervention; or decisions about who the perpetrator and victim are being based on the presentation of gender (Brown and Groscup 2009; Little and Terrance 2010; Pattavina et al. 2007; Poorman et al. 2003). An underlying assumption resulting from the public story of DVA is that 'mutual abuse' characterises the IPVA in LGB and/or T+ people's relationships. We return to this throughout the book.

Our analysis suggests that the public story of DVA should be developed to critique not only a female/male binary but also an ideal victim/perpetrator binary. Our qualitative analysis in Chap. 4 found evidence that recognition of victimisation can be impeded by individuals' beliefs that their own behaviours or demeanour do not correspond with their understanding of what constitutes a victim of DVA, especially if they have themselves enacted IPVA. Christie (1986) explains that victimhood is a socially constructed process that includes a judgement made and reinforced simultaneously by those victimised and by those whom the victimised turns to for help. If there is any scope for victim-blaming, evidence of provocation or agency, it is difficult to establish a credible 'ideal victim' identity, especially for those inhabiting minoritised identities (Donovan and Barnes 2018).

1.5.2 Relationship Rules and Practices of Love

Donovan and Hester (2014) argue that two 'relationship rules' are common in DVA relationships: the relationship is for the abusive partner and on their terms; and the victim/survivor is responsible for the abusive partner, their behaviour, the relationship, the household if they share one, and their children if they have any. They argue that these rules can be seen to mirror a dominant patriarchal heteronormatively (and we would add, cisnormatively) gendered discourse about intimacy in which one partner (typically embodied in an HC man) is the initiator who sets the terms for the relationship and makes all the key decisions, whilst the other partner (typically embodied in an HC woman) is the deferrer and enactor of the emotion work in the relationship. These roles cannot be easily read from the presentation of gender, especially in the relationships of LGB and/or T+ people, and are confused further by *practices of love*. That is, at key moments in DVA relationships, abusive partners express need or neediness to explain their abusive behaviours. This elicits emotion work from their partners, who are moved by their own love and/or the expressions of love from their abusive partner to forgive, protect, remain loyal and care for their abusive partners (Donovan and Hester 2011, 2014).

Practices of love turn the gender binary on its head as the abusive partner becomes emotionally needy, whilst the victim/survivor becomes emotionally responsible. Donovan and Hester (2011, 2014) argue that this has consequences for the victim/survivor's ability to recognise their victimisation. The relationship rules will often be evident in the accounts of the participants considered in Chap. 4. However, what we will also indicate is how, in more overt ways, cisnormative heteronormativity is expressed in experiences of coercive control by LGB and/or T+ participants. Whilst we present an argument that suggests more the similarities of experiences of IPVA across sexuality and gender identity because of the wider patriarchal context, we are attentive to the particular ways that this context shapes LGB and/or T+ people's unequal access to resources and opportunities, relative to their heterosexual, cisgender peers; and can be used by abusive partners to exert coercive control. We turn to this next.

1.6 The Context of Homo/Bi/Transphobia and Heterosexism and Its Consequences

The legislative landscape for those who identify as LGB and/or T+ has been positively transformed in the last nearly 20 years in the UK. Key milestones include the repeal (in Scotland in 2000 and the rest of the UK in 2003) of Section 28 of the *Local Government Act*. Passed in 1988, this made it illegal for local authorities to 'promote' homosexuality in schools and prevented schools from teaching about the 'pretend' families of lesbians and gay men. The *Adoption and Children's Act 2002* allowed same-sex couples to foster and adopt jointly and in 2013, same-sex marriage was legalised (but not in Northern Ireland). The *Equality Act 2010* requires equality of treatment in the provision of goods and services, and created the Equality Duty requiring publicly funded services to ensure that their provision is equally accessible across nine protected strands, among them, sexuality and transgender identity. Further protection is provided by the *Criminal Justice Act 2003*, which allows courts to attach enhanced sentences to convictions of offences motivated by homo/bi/transphobic hate.

The *Gender Recognition Act 2004* enables transgender people to apply to have their gender identity legally recognised. This legislation has recently been the subject of a government-led public consultation about ways of making the process easier to allow transgender people the right to self-identify their gender without having to provide evidence of, amongst other things, medical authenticity of their gender identity (Government Equalities Office [GEO] 2018a). There are particular problems facing victimised transgender women whose current or potential use of women-only refuges and rape crisis services has been subject to challenges which centre on the transphobic argument that trans women are not 'real women' and that they therefore pose a risk to the authentic, cisgender women using those services. The debate has been made difficult by some quite extreme positions taken by all sides (see The Guardian 2018). Such transphobic attitudes must only make it harder for transgender women and men to seek help as people who might have enacted violence and/or 'abusive' behaviours in their intimate relationships. Non-binary gendered people must also feel wary of approaching services shaped by a heteronormative, cisnormative approach to understanding IPVA.

Despite extensive legislative change, discrimination and hate towards LGB and/or T+ people remains prolific. The recent Metro (2016) research with young LGB and/or T+ people evidences widespread experiences of homo/bi/transphobia from their friends, family and neighbours and in school. Similarly, the GEO (2018b) *National LGBT Survey*, the largest survey of LGBT people anywhere in the world (n=108,100), found that 40% of respondents had experienced an incident (ranging from verbal abuse to sexual violence) in the 12 months prior to the survey from somebody they did not live with because they were LGBT. A recent Home Office study (O'Neill 2017) showed that there was a 27% increase in reports of hate crime on the grounds of sexuality and a 45% increase on the grounds of transgender identity between 2015/16 and 2016/17 in England and Wales. Two reasons are suggested for the increases across all hate crime protected characteristics: first, the impact of the 2016 referendum on whether the UK should leave the European Union; and second, improved police reporting systems. Increased reporting might also reflect the increased confidence of some of those victimised on the grounds of sexuality and/or transgender identity to report (Donovan et al. 2018).

There is also evidence that some faith-based groups will resist the introduction of mandatory inclusive relationships and sex education (RSE) in schools (Jenkins 2019; Rocker 2019); and it is as yet unclear how RSE will be LGB- and/or T+ inclusive (Formby and Donovan 2016). As this book is being written, there have been months of public demonstrations outside schools in Birmingham against the delivery of the 'No outsiders' programme which promotes sexualities equality and challenges homophobia in primary schools (Parveen 2019). The most recent *British Social Attitudes Survey* reports that the proportion of respondents agreeing that sex between two adults of the 'same sex' is 'not wrong at all' has dropped by two percentage points, from 68% to 66%. The authors suggest this reflects a plateau in the liberalisation of society because of a significant minority of faith-motivated respondents (Curtice et al. 2019). We next consider identity abuse as an outcome of this broader heterosexist and homo/bi/transphobic context in which LGB and/or T+ people live.

1.6.1 Identity Abuse

One difference between IPVA in LGB and/or T+ and cisgender heterosexual people's relationships is identity abuse. The potential for identity abuse derives from a societal context in which discriminatory, demeaning and undermining assumptions and stereotypes about gay men, lesbians, bisexual women and men, trans women and men, and non-binary gendered people are normalised. Such tropes can be used by abusive partners to control, punish, torment and/or deter from help-seeking and include, not exhaustively, threats to out partners to family, friends, employers, faith communities; threats to reveal or lie about a partner's HIV status; undermining a partner's sense of self-identity as an LGB and/or T+ person; refusing and/or controlling finances that are needed for transitioning; isolating partners from local LGBT scenes or events; creating fear that potential help providers will respond with homo/bi/transphobic discrimination to them and/or to the abusive partner (Brown 2011; Goldenberg et al. 2016; Hill et al. 2012; Ristock 2002). Those in their first relationship as a LGB and/or T+ person or with a T+ partner can be at particular risk of experiencing identity abuse (Brown 2011; Donovan and Hester 2014; McDonald 2012; Ristock 2002).

Donovan and Hester (2014) suggest that coming out can position somebody as 'younger' than a partner who has been out for some time. In the Coral Project we have extended this to talk about experiential power, where a more established, confident LGB and/or T+ person exploits a less established, newly out partner with their apparently superior knowledge about what it means to be authentically LGB and/or T+ (Donovan and Barnes in press; Donovan et al. 2014). Identity abuse is not particular to the IPVA relationships of LGB and/or T+ people (Donovan and Barnes in press): HC men similarly exploit social norms of HC femininity to control, punish and undermine their partners (Stark 2007). How identity abuse is enacted relies on the intersecting identities of both partners in the relationship, as is illustrated in the qualitative analysis in Chap. 4. Next, we return to the mainstream IPVA field to explain other conceptual tools that we use.

1.7   The Gender Symmetry/Asymmetry Debate as the Context for This Research

The problematisation of heteronormative, cisnormative gender by feminists is central to theorising in the mainstream field. Within the research focussing on IPVA in HC relationships, authors often introduce their work by positioning themselves and their analyses in relation to this explanatory framework to support or reject its premises. Dobash and Dobash (2004) characterise the two sides of this debate as 'family violence' and 'violence against women'.

Feminist violence against (HC) women researchers (e.g. Dobash and Dobash 2004; Johnson 1995, 2008; Stark 2007; Stark and Hester 2019; Walby et al. 2017) demonstrate that IPVA is gender asymmetrical—that is, perpetrated primarily by HC men towards HC women—and that it results from socially constructed, unequal, patriarchal relations played out in the private sphere that are supported, reflected and reinforced in the social systems of politics, law, the economy, and culture or civil society (Walby 1990). Conversely, family violence researchers demonstrate that IPVA is gender symmetrical—that is, equally likely to be perpetrated and experienced by HC men and HC women—although they often recognise that HC women disproportionately report severe injury and sexual violence (Hamby 2009; Straus 1999). However, they argue that the feminist emphasis on gender as an explanatory framework is ideologically driven, and acknowledge gender inequality as one of a number of causal factors, including dysfunctional family systems, and psycho-social factors such as stress (Gelles and Straus 1979; Straus 1999). This debate has deeply entrenched implications for knowledge production, and we return to it in Chap. 2.

1.7.1 Typologies of IPVA

Having argued for a more sociological approach to making sense of IPVA in the relationships of LGB and/or T+ people, we now turn to Johnson's seminal sociological work (1995, 2008, 2011; Kelly and Johnson 2008), which sets out a conceptually and empirically persuasive case for understanding the long-standing, often rancorous disagreements between the family violence and feminist approaches to IPVA. This work is central to our own because we believe that it provides conceptual tools that can be used as a starting point to making sense of IPVA, regardless of the sexuality or gender of the intimate partners. This requires studies to ask about a range of controlling behaviours, rather than only focussing on physical violence; to attempt to establish the direction of power; and to capture the motives, meanings and impacts of the behaviours experienced and/or used. Johnson's case—supported by empirical evidence from his own work (Johnson 2008) and that of others with HC women and HC men (Messinger et al. 2014; Myhill 2017)—is that family violence and feminist researchers are focussing on two different types of violence, due to the different methodologies and samples used.

Feminist researchers have conducted research predominantly with police data, crime surveys, accident and emergency and other health data, and populations using refuges and other crisis services, and have prioritised qualitative accounts from HC women (e.g. Hoff 1990; Kirkwood 1993; Wilcox 2006). This overwhelmingly yields knowledge about DVA, what Johnson calls coercively controlling violence (CCV, previously intimate terrorism), predominantly enacted by HC men towards HC women. Family violence researchers have conducted general population surveys and produced knowledge about what Johnson calls, 'situational couple violence' (SCV, previously 'common couple violence'), which can be enacted by either HC men or women. In subsequent research, Johnson and colleagues have identified three further types of violence: 'violent resistance' (VR), described as being predominantly the violence of HC women in response to the CCV of their HC male partners; 'mutual violent control', whereby both partners in an intimate relationship violently struggle for control; and 'separation-instigated violence', which is violence that starts when a partner reveals an intention to leave the relationship (Kelly and Johnson 2008).

The key distinction between these types of violence (which Johnson and his colleagues have predominantly defined as physical violence) hinges on the context of the violent incident, the motivation behind the violence, and whether there is intent to control the relationship at the general level (CCV) or it is a situation-specific incident in which the partner 'lashes out' in anger and/or in an attempt to control that specific situation (SCV). Johnson's later work recognises that physical violence does not need to be present, or needs to be so only minimally, for CCV to define the relationship dynamic (Johnson et al. 2014). Stark (2007) argues that coercive control provides the underlying motivation for physical violence. That CCV/DVA and SCV are distinct types of IPVA is shown not only in intent but also in the impacts. In their research, Leone et al. (2007) suggest that CCV has more negative impacts—on survivors' physical and mental health, their daily lives and their children. They find that survivors of CCV are more likely to seek help from the police or medical practitioners than those experiencing SCV; and that CCV, far more than SCV, can potentially escalate in severity of injury and consequences.

Others have since built on or extended Johnson's typology and have endeavoured to quantitatively measure coercive control independently from physical violence (e.g. Jasinski et al. 2014). Mennicke and Kulkarni (2016; see also Mennicke 2019) identified ten categories of IPVA in their study of ostensibly HC adult women and men by operationalising high/low-control categories intersecting with high/low-violence categories that take into account the direction of the violence and control. Hester et al. (2017) argue and demonstrate in their study of a clinical sample of HC men attending their general practitioner in England that whilst rates of physical violence might show gender symmetry, when measures of sexual violence along with coercive control are added to the overall picture of experiences, then gender asymmetry becomes stark. Messinger et al. (2018) focus on IPVA at the relationship rather than the individual level to better include recognition of coercive control, physical violence and the direction of each in the relationship. Thus, it has been demonstrated that coercive control may or may not include physical violence, echoing Stark (2007, 2010). We agree with the conclusions of these studies and critique the incident-based design of survey methodologies that characterise resistance as being 'in the moment' and against a particular incident of aggression or control. Instead, we suggest in Chap. 4 that resistance can also take the form of a relationship demeanour. Whether in the moment or as a demeanour, we refer to such IPVA as space for reaction (see below).

There have been critics of the shift in focus away from physical violence as the definer of DVA. Walby and Towers (2018) provide a comprehensive critique of coercive control that begins with their argument that, methodologically, a focus on what they call domestic violence crime (crimes related to physical violence, sexual violence and stalking) and serious injury are the most reliable measures to use in population surveys.

Our response to their work (Donovan and Barnes 2019) illustrates how their approach continues to make invisible the experiences of LGB and/ or T+ people and outlines our counter-argument that including coercive control is fundamental to making sense of whether and how power operates in relationships where IPVA occurs. We argue that this is crucial to ensure that those using physical violence in self-defence, protection of property, pets or children, or in retaliation are not counted and addressed as if they are the same as those who enact DVA.

It is Johnson's typology that we draw on in making sense of our quantitative and qualitative data (see Chaps. 3, 4 and 5) about experiences of IPVA in the relationships of LGB and/or T+ people. However, we also keep in mind that typologies of IPVA can be problematic (Kelly and Johnson 2008). Walby and Towers (2018) critique them for their reliance on static concepts of violence, rather than dynamic concepts that recognise the possibility of escalation both between types of violence (e.g. from SCV to CCV) and within types of violence (although Johnson [in Leone et al. 2007] does talk about escalation occurring in SCV, but not to the same extent as in CCV). Walby and Towers (2018) argue that early intervention should be a practice response to cases of IPVA assessed as low risk in order to prevent them from escalating to high risk (see also Donovan et al. 2010). Others have also critiqued the way risk assessments based on the experiences of HC women have been unproblematically adopted for universal use, regardless of their appropriateness for survivors in same-sex relationships (Donovan 2013; Robinson and Rowlands 2009). The same critiques can be applied to Johnson's typology. The point made is that neither risk nor typologies of violence are neutral concepts, but are constituted through knowledge based on the experiences of HC women (Donovan 2013).

Risk assessment tools, like binaries and typologies, can become essentialising in application. The defining criteria can become sedimented and/or reified into a static profile that fixes an 'extreme', 'typical' or 'prototype' as representative of the 'truth' about that type, binary or risk level (see Walklate and Mythen 2011). The problem of extremes is an important one in the field of IPVA. Johnson (2008) argues that control is a continuum, yet typologies can 'force' decisions towards extreme cases. This belies what authors such as Hodes and Mennicke (2019) and Stark

(2007) argue, which is that most DVA is low level and chronic, stretching across the relationship, rather than being experienced in acute or escalating crisis situations. Typologies can only be useful if they are understood as contingent and used as a guide to indicate whether there is a direction of power in the relationship context and its impact. However, if rigidly applied in practice settings, there is a danger that, when people do not 'fit', their safety and well-being can be jeopardised by a lack of appropriate response. We return to this in Chap. 5. This has happened to some extent with the assumption often made that IPVA in the relationships of LGB and/or T+ people is 'mutual abuse'.

1.7.2 Telling a Different Story About 'Mutual Abuse'

The notion that there is an equality in the relationships of LGB and/or T+ people because of the apparent absence of patriarchal, heteronormative, cisgendered inequalities has fuelled an assumption that IPVA in these relationships must be low-risk 'mutual abuse' or 'bi-directional violence' (see Baker et al. 2013; Duke and Davidson 2009; Hodes and Mennicke 2019; Messinger 2017; Ristock 2002; and Johnson in his early work 1995). This is despite little research focussing on this, and where research has recorded and analysed the motives for the 'abusive' behaviours, the proportion of mutual abuse has been very small (e.g. Donovan and Hester 2014).

Messinger (2017, 2018) has troubled the assumptions made about mutual abuse in the relationships of LGB and/or T+ people and usefully highlights the methodological problems with much of the (predominantly North American) quantitative research conducted in this area. A main problem is that research designs often use a time period rather than a relationship context as the framework for questions asked about whether and which violent/'abusive' behaviours have been experienced and/or enacted by survey respondents. However, a time period framework might conflate different relationships as a single one. For example, Kelly et al.'s (2011) study of 'mutual partner violence' and substance use in the relationships of urban LGB participants uses different time periods for physical violence from a 'primary partner' (the last five years) and substance use (the last three months). It is not clear whether the primary partner is the same across the five years asked about, or whether the substance use indicated in the previous three months reflects the participant's substance use over the previous five years. A time period of only a year can still lead to unreliable assumptions being made about reports of IPVA in the same relationship, especially with adolescent young people (see Messinger et al. 2018). The additional problem, as we see it, is the inclination of researchers to operationalise 'mutual abuse' as if the violence and 'abusive' behaviours being reported are always the same in motive, intent and impact. For example, whilst Bartholomew et al. (2008) acknowledged that they were not able to report on motives for the perpetration reported, they argued that because the levels of victimisation and perpetration were very similar, this did not reflect a 'stereotypical batterer/victim pattern' in which a victim might occasionally react in self-defence (Bartholomew et al. 2008, p. 633). We return to this in Chap. 4 to illustrate that regular incidents of apparently mutual abuse might be part of a coercively controlling relationship.

Frankland and Brown (2014) have conducted one of the first analyses of IPVA in same-sex relationships, building on Johnson's typology to include non-violent control. They conclude that 'coercive control represents one of the core features of IPV, regardless of gender' (Frankland and Brown 2014, p. 21). They also found that 12.5% of their sample of 184 reported 'mutual violent control' but because they do not research motives, meanings, context and/or impact of the behaviours they measure as part of mutual violent control, it is difficult to understand how they are operationalising an understanding of power in their work. As we suggest next and illustrate in Chap. 4, understanding how power operates in a relationship context rather than during a specific incident is critical, especially when both partners appear to be experiencing and enacting violence and 'abusive' behaviours.

1.7.3   Space for Reaction

As a contribution to the debate on mutual abuse, we propose a new term for understanding how those victimised by DVA might use IPVA. 'Space for action' (see Kelly 2003; Sharp-Jeffs et al. 2018; Wilcox 2006), based on the experiences of HC women, conveys the ability of those victimised by DVA to make autonomous decisions. As such, space for action puts the needs, desires, ambition, and goals of the victimised partner at the centre of assessments of the degree to which they are liberated or entrapped during and following a DVA relationship. In this book, we offer 'space for reaction' as a term that describes the range of ways that those victimised by DVA respond or react to the coercively controlling and violent behaviours of their partners. This does not refer to behaviours that increase the outward-facing freedoms and autonomy of the victimised partner conveyed in space for action, but are, rather, responses to violent and abusive partners that attempt to (re-)establish a more egalitarian power relationship. This can include physical violence used in self-defence and/or to protect others and property, or to retaliate or punish a violent and abusive partner; and a range of non-physically violent behaviours that attempt to resist the power and control of their partner and/or re-balance (albeit not necessarily successfully) the power relations in the relationship; and their help-seeking behaviours. We return to this in Chap. 4.

1.8 Telling an Ecological, Intersectional Story

Our conceptual approach is informed by Heise's ecological framework (see Donovan and Barnes in press). Heise draws from the work of Bronfenbrenner (1979, in Heise 1998) and Carlson (1984), who developed a model for understanding behaviour that incorporates the various layers of influence that shape and produce an individual's behaviour: their biography and history; their family and immediate community; the broader sociocultural context; and the broader social-structural context. Heise (1998) employs this approach to bring together what is known about violence against women. Her ecological model has nested layers to indicate that they overlap and interconnect, reinforcing and constructing each other. In our analysis we similarly examine how cisgendered heteronormativity, and heterosexism and cisgenderism (re)produce and reinforce the invisibility of IPVA in the relationships of LGB and/or T+ people at both macro and micro levels, and how this is experienced and/

or anticipated in different ways, depending on individuals' intersecting identities and co-membership of different social groups. This is especially pertinent when we examine help-seeking experiences and barriers in Chap. 5 (see also Donovan and Barnes in press).

Finally, our analysis is shaped by our experience of researching the lives of LGB and/or T+ people, which tells us that categories of sexuality and gender are not stable but fluid, and that gender is not the only or, necessarily, the most important lens through which to make sense of IPVA (Donovan and Barnes 2019). Like Ristock (2005), we argue that the rigid fixation on gender as the sole lens through which to examine IPVA can be understood as essentialist. An intersectional analysis facilitates an exploration of the simultaneous impacts that arise from living in a society organised around structural hierarchies that result from patriarchy, post-colonialism and capitalism (Crenshaw 1991; Walby 2007). In the Coral Project, intersecting identities of sex, gender, sexuality, 'race', faith, social class, disability, age, and experience of being out as an LGB and/or T+ person were pertinent. As we demonstrate throughout the analysis in this book, LGB and/or T+ people's multiple, intersecting identities impact on their reported experiences and enactment of IPVA, their recognition of DVA, their decisions regarding help-seeking and the ways in which others external to the relationship perceive them and what is happening in their relationship.

1.9 Summary

This chapter has set out the aims of the book and its terms of reference including establishing our disciplinary origins in sociology and an outline of the key sociological concepts that we adopt throughout the book. We have provided a brief overview of the research on IPVA in the relationships of LGB and/or T+ people; a rationale for why we do not dismiss feminist theorising in making sense of this; and why we draw on Johnson's typology of IPVA to analyse our data. The impact of the public story of DVA on the way in which IPVA in the relationships of LGB and/or T+ people is often characterised as mutual abuse and why this might be has been outlined. We expanded the public story of DVA to include how a binary of victim/perpetrator overlaid on the HC female/male binary can prevent those who are being victimised and using IPVA from recognising their experiences as victims. Relatedly, we proposed 'space for reaction' as a term to convey the violent and non-violent behaviours which victimised partners might engage in as a response to the DVA they are experiencing, in order to try to (re-)establish a more egalitarian relationship dynamic. Finally, we described our intersectional approach to analysing our data as part of an ecological approach that not only accounts for the multiple identities inhabited by participants, but also the wider cultural and social institutional impacts that reproduce structural inequalities.

In the following chapter the Coral Project methodology is explained, and Chap. 3 begins to queer the narratives that quantitative data can produce, not only about IPVA in the relationships of LGB and/or T+ people but more generally. In Chap. 4 we draw on five qualitative case studies to critically explore what might be seen as mutual abuse in the relationships of LGB and/or T+ people and expand on the concept of space for reaction to take account of the use of IPVA by those being victimised by DVA. Chapter 5 concentrates on help-seeking and our contention that what is needed is a much wider 'relationships services' approach to providing support for intimate relationships and preventing IPVA. Finally, Chap. 6 draws together our main messages and makes the point that whilst our focus has been on the relationships of LGB and/or T+ people, many of our conclusions are applicable to the mainstream field of IPVA, both in research and in practice.

References

Bachman, C. L., & Gooch, B. (2018). *LGBT in Britain: Trans report*. London: Stonewall and YouGov.

Baker, N. L., Buick, J. D., Kim, S. R., Moniz, S., & Nava, K. L. (2013). Lessons from examining same-sex intimate partner violence. *Sex Roles: A Journal of Research, 69*(3–4), 182–192.

Balsam, K. F., & Szymanski, D. M. (2005). Relationship quality and domestic violence in women's same-sex relationships: The role of minority stress. *Psychology of Women Quarterly, 29*, 258–269.

Bartholomew, K., Regan, K., Oram, D., & White, M. (2008). Correlates in partner abuse in male same-sex relationships. *Violence and Victims, 23*(3), 344–360.

Brown, M. J., & Groscup, J. (2009). Perceptions of same-sex domestic violence among crisis centre staff. *Journal of Family Violence, 24,* 87–93.

Brown, N. (2011). Holding tensions of victimisation and perpetration: Partner abuse in trans communities. In J. Ristock (Ed.), *Intimate partner violence in LGBTQ lives.* London: Routledge.

Cannon, C., & Buttell, F. (2015). Illusion of inclusion: The failure of the gender paradigm to account for intimate partner violence in LGBT relationships. *Partner Abuse, 6*(1), 65–77.

Carlson, B. (1984). Causes and maintenance of domestic violence: An ecological analysis. *Social Service Review, 58,* 569–587.

Carvalho, A. F., Lewis, R. J., Derlega, V. J., Winstead, B. A., & Viggiano, C. (2011). Internalized sexual minority stressors and same-sex intimate partner violence. *Journal of Family Violence, 26,* 501–509.

Christie, N. (1986). The ideal victim. In E. Fattah (Ed.), *From crime policy to victim policy: Reorienting the justice system* (pp. 17–30). Basingstoke: Macmillan.

Crenshaw, K. (1991). Mapping the margins: Intersectionality, identity politics, and violence against women of color. *Stanford Law Review, 43*(6), 1241–1299.

Curtice, J., Clery, E., Perry, J., Phillips, M., & Rahim, N. (Eds.). (2019). *British social attitudes: The 36th report.* London: National Centre for Social Research.

Dobash, R. E., & Dobash, R. P. (1979). *Violence against wives: A case against the patriarchy.* New York: Free Press.

Dobash, R. P., & Dobash, R. E. (2004). Women's violence to men in intimate relationships: Working on a puzzle. *British Journal of Criminology, 44*(3), 324–349.

Donovan, C. (2013). Redefining domestic violence and abuse: Unintended consequences of risk assessment. In J. Kearney & C. Donovan (Eds.), *Constructing risky identities in policy and practice* (pp. 109–126). Basingstoke: Palgrave Macmillan.

Donovan, C. (2015). Tackling inequality in the intimate sphere: Problematizing love and violence in same-sex relationships. In R. Leckey (Ed.), *After legal equality* (pp. 167–183). Oxon: Routledge.

Donovan, C., & Barnes, R. (2018). Becoming 'ideal' or falling short?: The legitimacy of lesbian, gay, bisexual and/or transgender victims of domestic violence and hate crime. In M. Duggan (Ed.), *Revisiting the ideal victim concept* (pp. 83–102). Policy Press: Bristol.

Donovan, C., & Barnes, R. (2019, July 26). Re-tangling the concept of coercive control: A view from the margins and a response to Walby and Towers (2018). *Criminology and Criminal Justice.* https://doi.org/10.1177/1748895819864622

Donovan, C., & Barnes, R. (in press). Help-seeking among lesbian, gay, bisexual and/or transgender victims/survivors of domestic violence and abuse: The impacts of cisgendered heteronormativity and invisibility. *Journal of Sociology.* https://doi.org/10.1177/1440783319882088

Donovan, C., Barnes, R., & Nixon, C. (2014). *The Coral Project: Exploring abusive behaviours in lesbian, gay, bisexual and/or transgender relationships: Interim report.* Sunderland and Leicester: University of Sunderland and University of Leicester. Retrieved March 30, 2019, from https://www2.le.ac.uk/departments/criminology/documents/coral-project-interim-report

Donovan, C., Clayton, J., & Macdonald, S. (2018, September 28). New directions in hate reporting research: Agency, heterogeneity and relationality. *Sociological Research Online.* https://doi.org/10.1177/1360780418798848

Donovan, C., Griffiths, S., Groves, N., with Johnson, H., & Douglass, J. (2010). *Making connections count: An evaluation of early intervention models for change in domestic violence, 2004–2009.* Sunderland: University of Sunderland.

Donovan, C., & Hester, M. (2010). 'I hate the word "victim"': An exploration of recognition of domestic violence in same sex relationships. *Social Policy and Society, 9*(2), 279–289.

Donovan, C., & Hester, M. (2011). Exploring emotion work in domestically abusive relationships. In J. Ristock (Ed.), *Intimate partner violence in LGBTQ lives* (pp. 81–101). New York and Abingdon: Routledge.

Donovan, C., & Hester, M. (2014). *Domestic violence and sexuality: What's love got to do with it?* Bristol: Policy Press.

Duke, A., & Davidson, M. M. (2009). Same-Sex intimate partner violence: Lesbian, gay and bisexual affirmative outreach and advocacy. *Journal of Aggression, Maltreatment and Trauma, 18*(8), 795–816.

Edwards, K. M., Sylaska, K. M., & Neal, A. M. (2015). Intimate partner violence among sexual minority populations: A critical review of the literature and agenda for future research. *Psychology of Violence, 5*(2), 112–121.

Finneran, C., & Stephenson, R. (2012). Intimate partner violence among men who have sex with men: A systematic review. *Trauma, Violence, & Abuse, 14*(2), 168–185.

Formby, E., & Donovan, C. (2016). *Selfies evaluation. Final report.* Sheffield: Sheffield Hallam University.

Frankland, A., & Brown, J. (2014). Coercive control in same-sex intimate partner violence. *Journal of Family Violence, 29*(1), 15–22.

Gelles, R. J., & Straus, M. A. (1979). Violence in the Family. *Journal of Social Issues., 35*(2), 15–39.

Goldenberg, T., Stephenson, R., Freeland, R., Finneran, C., & Hadley, C. (2016). 'Struggling to be the alpha': Sources of tension and intimate partner violence in same-sex relationships between men. *Culture, Health & Sexuality, 18*(8), 875–889.

Government Equalities Office (GEO). (2018a). Reform of the Gender Recognition Act–Government Consultation. Retrieved September 10, 2019, from https://www.gov.uk/government/consultations/reform-of-the-gender-recognition-act-2004

Government Equalities Office (GEO). (2018b). *National LGBT Survey: Research report*. London: Crown Copyright.

Guadalupe-Diaz, X. L., & Jasinski, J. (2017). I wasn't a priority, I wasn't a victim': Challenges in help seeking for transgender survivors of intimate partner violence. *Violence Against Women, 23*(6), 772–792.

Hamby, S. (2009). The gender debate about intimate partner violence: Solutions and dead ends. *Psychological Trauma: Theory, Research, Practice, and Policy, 1*(1), 24–34.

Hassouneh, D., & Glass, N. (2008). The influence of gender role stereotyping on women's experiences of female same-sex intimate partner violence. *Violence Against Women, 14*(3), 310–325.

Head, S., & Milton, M. (2014). Filling the silence: Exploring the bisexual experience of intimate partner abuse. *Journal of Bisexuality, 14*, 277–299.

Heise, L. L. (1998). Violence against women: An integrated, ecological framework. *Violence Against Women, 4*(3), 262–290.

Hester, M., Jones, C., Williamson, E., Fahmy, E., & Feder, G. (2017). Is it coercive controlling violence? A cross-sectional domestic violence and abuse survey of men attending general practice in England. *Psychology of Violence, 7*(3), 417–427.

Hill, N., Woodson, K., Ferguson, A., & Parks, C., Jr. (2012). Intimate partner abuse among African American lesbians: Prevalence, risk factors, theory, and resilience. *Journal of Family Violence, 27*(5), 401–413.

Hodes, C., & Mennicke, A. (2019). Is it conflict or abuse? A practice note for furthering differential assessment and response. *Journal of Clinical Social Work, 47*(2), 176–184.

Hoff, L. A. (1990). *Battered women as survivors*. London and New York: Routledge.

Home Office. (2013). *Correspondence. Circular 003/2013: New government domestic violence and abuse definition.* Retrieved January 29, 2019, from https://www.gov.uk/government/publications/new-government-domestic-violence-and-abuse-definition/circular-0032013-new-government-domestic-violence-and-abuse-definition

Jamieson, L. (1998). *Intimacy and personal relationships in modern society.* Cambridge: Polity Press.

Jasinski, J., Blumenstein, L., & Morgan, R. (2014). Testing Johnson's typology: Is there gender symmetry in intimate terrorism? *Violence and Victims, 29*(1), 73–88.

Jenkins, S. (2019, March 30). Sex education is not a matter for ministers. *The Guardian.*

Johnson, M. P. (1995). Patriarchal terrorism and common couple violence: Two forms of violence against women. *Journal of Marriage and Family, 57*(2), 283–294.

Johnson, M. P. (2008). *A typology of domestic violence: Intimate terrorism, violent resistance, and situational couple violence.* Boston: Northeastern University Press.

Johnson, M. P. (2011). Gender and types of intimate partner violence: A response to an anti-feminist literature review. *Aggression and Violent Behavior, 16*(4), 289–296.

Johnson, M. P., & Ferraro, K. J. (2000). Research on domestic violence in the 1990s: Making distinctions. *Journal of Marriage and the Family, 62*(4), 948–963.

Johnson, M. P., Leone, J. M., & Xu, Y. (2014). Intimate terrorism and situational couple violence in general surveys: Ex-spouses required. *Violence Against Women, 20*(2), 186–207.

Kelly, B. C., Izienici, H., Bimbi, D. S., & Parsons, J. T. (2011). The intersection of mutual partner violence and substance use among urban gays, lesbians, and bisexuals. *Deviant Behavior, 32*, 379–404.

Kelly, J. B., & Johnson, M. P. (2008). Differentiation among types of intimate partner violence: Research update and implications for interventions. *Family Court Review, 46*(3), 476–499.

Kelly, L. (2003). The wrong debate: Reflections on why force is not the key issue with respect to trafficking in women for sexual exploitation. *Feminist Review, 73*, 139–144.

Kimmes, J., Mallory, A., Spencer, C., Beck, A., Cafferky, B., & Stith, S. (2019). A meta-analysis of risk markers for intimate partner violence in same-sex relationships. *Trauma, Violence, & Abuse, 20*(3), 374–384.

Kirkwood, C. (1993). *Leaving abusive partners: From the scars of survival to the wisdom for change*. London: Sage.

Leone, J. M., Johnson, M. P., & Cohan, C. M. (2007). Victim help-seeking: Differences between intimate terrorism and situational couple violence. *Family Relations, 56*(5), 427–439.

Little, B., & Terrance, C. (2010). Perceptions of domestic violence in lesbian relationships: Stereotypes and gender role expectations. *Journal of Homosexuality, 57*, 429–440.

Mason, T. B., Lewis, R. J., Milletich, R. J., Kelly, M. L., Minifie, J. B., & Derlega, D. J. (2014). Psychological aggression in lesbian, gay, and bisexual individuals' intimate relationships: A review of prevalence, correlates, and measurement issues. *Aggression and Violent Behaviour, 19*, 219–234.

McDonald, C. (2012). The social context of woman-to-woman intimate partner abuse (WWIPA). *Journal of Family Violence, 27*(7), 635–645.

Mendoza, J. (2011). The impact of minority stress on gay male partner abuse. In J. Ristock (Ed.), *Intimate partner violence in LGBTQ lives* (pp. 169–181). New York and Abingdon: Routledge.

Mennicke, A. (2019). Expanding and validating a typology of intimate partner violence: Intersections of violence and control within relationships. *Violence Against Women, 25*(4), 379–400.

Mennicke, A., & Kulkarni, S. (2016). Understanding gender symmetry within an expanded partner violence typology. *Journal of Family Violence, 31*, 1013–1018.

Messinger, A. M. (2017). *LGBTQ intimate partner violence: Lessons for policy, practice, and research*. Oakland, CA: University of California Press.

Messinger, A. M. (2018). Bidirectional same-gender and sexual minority intimate partner violence. *Violence and Gender, 5*(4), 241–249.

Messinger, A. M., Fry, D. A., Rickert, V. I., Catallozzi, M., & Davidson, L. L. (2014). Extending Johnson's intimate partner violence typology: Lessons from an adolescent sample. *Violence Against Women, 20*(8), 948–971.

Messinger, A. M., Sessarego, S. N., Edwards, K. M., & Banyard, V. L. (2018). Bidirectional IPV among adolescent sexual minorities. *Journal of Interpersonal Violence*. https://doi.org/10.1177/0886260518807218

Metro. (2016). *Youth chances: Integrated report*. London: Metro Charity.

Mills, C. W. (1959). *The sociological imagination*. New York and Oxford: Oxford University Press.

Myhill, A. (2017). Measuring domestic violence: Context is everything. *Journal of Gender-Based Violence, 1*, 33–44.

O'Neill, A. (2017). *Hate crime, England and Wales, 2016/17*. London: Crown Copyright.

Office for National Statistics (ONS). (2015). *Sexual identity by age group by country*. London: ONS.

Office for National Statistics (ONS). (2018). *Women most at risk of experiencing partner abuse in England and Wales: Years ending March 2015 to 2017*. London: ONS.

Oringher, J., & Samuelson, K. (2011). Intimate partner violence and the role of masculinity in male same-sex relationships. *Traumatology, 17*(2), 68–74.

Parveen, N. (2019, March 4). Birmingham school stops LGBT lessons after parents protest. *The Guardian*.

Pattavina, A., Hirschel, D., Buzawa, E., Faggiani, D., & Bentley, H. (2007). A comparison of the police response to heterosexual versus same-sex intimate partner violence. *Violence Against Women, 13*(4), 374–394.

Poorman, P. B., Seelau, E. P., & Seelau, S. M. (2003). Perceptions of domestic abuse in same-sex relationships and implications for criminal justice and mental health responses. *Violence and Victims, 18*(6), 659–669.

Renzetti, C. M. (1992). *Violent betrayal: Partner abuse in lesbian relationships*. London: Sage.

Ristock, J. (2002). *No more secrets: Violence in lesbian relationships*. London and New York: Routledge.

Ristock, J. (2005). Relationship violence in lesbian/gay/bisexual/transgender/queer [LGBTQ] communities: Moving beyond a gender-based framework. Retrieved September 27, 2019, from http://citeseerx.ist.psu.edu/viewdoc/download?doi=10.1.1.208.7282&rep=rep1&type=pdf

Ristock, J. (2011). Introduction: Intimate partner violence in LGBTQ lives. In J. Ristock (Ed.), *Intimate partner violence in LGBTQ lives*. New York and Abingdon: Routledge.

Robinson, A. L., & Rowlands, J. (2009). Assessing and managing risk among different victims of domestic abuse: Limits of a generic model of risk assessment? *Security Journal, 22*, 190–204.

Rocker, S. (2019, February 26). 'Sex education plans will "limit" parents' religious rights', say opponents. *The Jewish Chronicle*. Online. Retrieved March 30, 2019, from https://www.thejc.com/education/education-news/sex-education-proposals-opposed-1.481183

Seidman, S., Meeks, C., & Traschen, F. (1999). Beyond the closet? The changing social meaning of homosexuality in the United States. *Sexualities, 2*, 9–34.

Sharp-Jeffs, N., Kelly, L., & Klein, R. (2018). Long journeys toward freedom: The relationship between coercive control and space for action: Measurement and emerging evidence. *Violence Against Women, 24*(2), 163–185.

Stark, E. (2007). *Coercive control: How men entrap women in personal life*. Oxford: Oxford University Press.

Stark, E. (2010). Do violent acts equal abuse? Resolving the gender parity/asymmetry dilemma. *Sex Roles, 62*, 201–211.

Stark, E., & Hester, M. (2019). Coercive control: Update and review. *Violence Against Women, 25*(1), 81–104.

Straus, M. A. (1999). The controversy over domestic violence by women: A methodological, theoretical, and sociology of science analysis. In X. B. Arriaga & S. Oskamp (Eds.), *Violence in intimate relationships* (pp. 17–44). London: Sage.

The Guardian. (2018, October 17). The Guardian view on the Gender Recognition Act: Where rights collide. *The Guardian*.

Toro-Alfonso, J., & Rodriguez-Madera, S. (2004). Domestic violence in Puerto Rican gay male couples: Perceived prevalence, intergenerational violence, addictive behaviors, and conflict resolution skills. *Journal of Interpersonal Violence, 19*(6), 639–654.

Walby, S. (1990). *Theorizing patriarchy*. Oxford: Blackwell.

Walby, S. (2007). Complexity theory, systems theory, and multiple intersecting social inequalities. *Philosophy of the Social Sciences, 37*(4), 449–470.

Walby, S., & Towers, J. (2018). Untangling the concept of coercive control: Theorizing domestic violent crime. *Criminology and Criminal Justice, 18*(1), 7–28.

Walby, S., Towers, J., Balderston, S., Corradi, C., Francis, B., Heiskanen, M., Helweg-Larsen, K., Mergaert, L., Olive, P., Palmer, E., Stöckl, H., & Strid, S. (2017). *The concept and measurement of violence against women and men*. Bristol: Policy Press.

Walklate, S., & Mythen, G. (2011). Beyond risk theory: Experiential knowledge and 'knowing otherwise'. *Criminology and Criminal Justice, 11*(2), 99–113.

Walters, M. L., Chen, J., & Breiding, M. J. (2013). *The National Intimate Partner and Sexual Violence Survey (NISVS): 2010 findings on victimization by sexual orientation*. Atlanta: National Center for Injury Prevention and Control, Centers for Disease Control and Prevention.

Wilcox, P. (2006). *Surviving domestic violence: Gender, poverty and agency*. Basingstoke: Palgrave Macmillan.

Wu, E., El-Bassel, N., McVinney, D., Hess, L., Fopeano, M. V., Hwang, H. G., Charania, M., & Mansergh, G. (2014). The association between substance use and intimate partner violence within black male same-sex relationships. *Journal of Interpersonal Violence, 30*(5), 762–781.

2

Producing Stories About Intimate Partner Violence and Abuse: The Coral Project Methodology

Abstract Chapter 2 focusses on the dominant methodologies for producing knowledge about intimate partner violence and abuse (IPVA), before offering a discussion and justification of the innovative methodology adopted for the mixed-methods Coral Project research. We argue that it is necessary to trouble, or queer, both the reproduction of simplistic binaries of male/female and victim/perpetrator and the invisibility of LGB and/or T+ people in the mainstream heteronormative, cisnormative IPVA literature. In particular, we critique the Conflict Tactics Scale (CTS) and emphasise the importance of capturing the contexts in which violence and 'abusive' behaviours are experienced and used. We demonstrate how our Coral Project methodology, which employed both an LGB and/or T+ population survey and follow-up qualitative interviews, sought to overcome some of the limitations of existing approaches. We explain the approach that we took to recruit as diverse a sample as we could, as well as the ethical and safety considerations that this research necessitated. Paving the way for the analysis which follows, we illustrate how the triangulation of quantitative and qualitative data can trouble simplistic readings of quantitative data.

© The Author(s) 2020

C. Donovan, R. Barnes, *Queering Narratives of Domestic Violence and Abuse*, Palgrave Studies in Victims and Victimology, https://doi.org/10.1007/978-3-030-35403-9_2

Keywords Coercive control • Data analysis • Domestic violence and abuse • Measuring intimate partner violence and abuse • Methodology • Mixed-methods • Perpetrators • Qualitative interviews • Research ethics • Survey design

2.1   Introduction

This chapter has two objectives. The first is to critique dominant methodologies for producing knowledge about intimate partner violence and abuse (IPVA), primarily with reference to the mainstream heteronormative, cisnormative IPVA literature. In particular, we trouble, or more aptly, queer, the tendency in more positivistic IPVA research to reproduce the simplistic binaries that we have already outlined (male/female, victim/perpetrator), which overcome the analytical inconvenience of nuance and fluidity. The second is to present the Coral Project's innovative methodology for researching IPVA victimisation and perpetration in LGB and/or T+ people's relationships. As we shall explain, our methodology sought to capture more nuanced data about the use of violence and 'abusive' behaviours by a population that is almost exclusively hidden. Our mixed-methods approach enables a degree of triangulation which reveals the limitations of quantitative data alone, even when using a more complex and nuanced survey tool. One of the most illuminating questions that we address is: how might our claims and conclusions differ if we had not collected complementary qualitative data? We provide examples from our data to show the disjunctures and misunderstandings which the triangulation of quantitative and qualitative data reveals.

2.2   Researching IPVA: Methods and Measures

Chapter 1 outlined how much IPVA research has coalesced around the gender (a)symmetry debate between feminist and family violence researchers, fuelling many methodological debates. For ourselves, as researchers of IPVA in a population that is largely marginal to these debates, three issues need to be highlighted:

1. How IPVA is defined and conceptualised
2. The merits and limitations of different methodologies and measures for knowledge production about IPVA
3. Sampling and the heteronormative, cisnormative assumption that pervades most IPVA research

These issues structure our troubling—or queering—of dominant modes of knowledge production in the mainstream heteronormative, cisnormative IPVA literature, and critically inform how we designed the Coral Project's methodology.

2.2.1   How IPVA Is Defined and Conceptualised

One of the challenges in IPVA research is that there is no universal definition of IPVA, and the various, existing, definitions and understandings shift temporally and geographically. Nevertheless, the key distinctions can be distilled down to three key considerations. The first is whether a broad or narrow definition is applied (Bender 2017; DeKeseredy and Schwartz 2011). This primarily relates to whether IPVA is restricted to physical violence and/or the most serious or criminal forms of sexual violence (as advocated by Straus 1999; Walby and Towers 2018), or whether a wider range of psychological, emotional, sexual and financial behaviours are recognised, as was the case in the Coral Project.

Arguments against broadening the definition of IPVA point to the dangers of diluting understandings of IPVA (Walby and Towers 2018) and the difficulties of measuring emotional abuse (Karakurt and Silver 2013). It is unsurprising, therefore, that narrower definitions tend to result in lower rates of reported victimisation (DeKeseredy and Schwartz 2011). Yet, given that newer understandings of coercive control emphasise that incidents of physical violence may be relatively infrequent, it is an oversight not to attempt to capture the multiple and more nuanced ways in which 'micro-regulation' (Stark 2007) of victims'/survivors' daily lives occurs (DeKeseredy and Schwartz 2011; Donovan and Barnes 2019; Myhill 2017; Myhill and Kelly 2019).

A second, related consideration is whether researchers afford participants the opportunity to identify forms of abuse which fall outside the researcher's operationalisation of IPVA (Bender 2017). Providing this opportunity is more consistent with a feminist methodological approach which values women's voices and challenges the hierarchical researcher-researched relationship whereby the all-knowing researcher imposes their preordained categories onto passive research participants (Acker et al. 1983; Gavey 1999). In the Coral Project we included a large number of violent potentially 'abusive' behaviours (70 items for victimisation and 69 items for perpetration), organised under the four sub-categories of physical, emotional, sexual and financial behaviour. At the end of each section, free-text options invited further information that respondents considered relevant.

A third consideration relates to language. Even when measuring the same phenomenon, the language used when operationalising concepts can affect rates of reporting. Rape is a key example: asking respondents whether they have been 'raped' by a partner will yield a lower rate of reporting when compared with asking about experiences of specific non-consensual sexual acts (Gavey 1999; Jaquier et al. 2010; Walby and Myhill 2001). Piloting of the survey instruments to check that terminology had been communicated clearly (Ruel et al. 2016), and that questions were understood as intended by the research team, was incorporated into the Coral Project's methodology.

2.2.2   Methodologies and Measures for Producing Knowledge About IPVA

Whichever definition of IPVA is adopted, the next step is to operationalise it so that appropriate data collection tools can be developed. Quantitative methods—especially studies aimed at determining prevalence, or identifying correlations or causal relationships—dominate the IPVA field internationally. Therefore, various measures of IPVA have developed and been widely replicated with different (usually heterosexual, cisgender [HC]) samples. Whilst Bender (2017) provides a more comprehensive review and critique of different measures, the measure which we focus on here is the Conflict Tactics Scale (CTS), which is the most replicated instrument to date for use with intimate partners to measure conflict resolution (Straus 2005).

The CTS was first developed by Murray Straus for the National Family Violence Surveys (NFVS) in 1975 and 1985 in the USA with randomly selected samples of married people. Respondents are asked to indicate which of the listed conflict tactics they have experienced and used in the last 12 months or ever, and how frequently (ranging from never to more than 20 times) in the last 12 months (Straus 1979). In response to criticisms of the CTS, the revised CTS-2 was developed in the mid-1990s (Straus et al. 1996). Key changes included the addition of a scale to measure experiences and perpetration of sexual coercion, and a scale to measure physical injuries resulting from assaults. In total, there are 78 items in the CTS-2: 39 pertaining to the respondent's own behaviour or injuries and 39 pertaining to their partner's.

Since their development, the CTS, CTS-2 and modified versions thereof have consistently found that women and men use violence to similar extents (see Dobash et al. 1992; Loseke and Kurz 2005; Nicholls and Dutton 2001; Saunders 2002; Straus 2005), and sometimes that women use some violent conflict tactics at higher rates than men (Archer 2002; Straus 2004). However, the CTS also consistently finds that women are much more likely to sustain injuries as a result of their male spouse or partner's assaults, leading Straus to argue that the main concern with women's violence is its potential to provoke more harmful and injurious assaults from men (Straus 1999, 2005).

Despite the amendments, the CTS remains widely critiqued (Currie 1998; Dobash et al. 1992; Kimmel 2002; Loseke and Kurz 2005) because of its bluntness as a measurement tool, its limited measurement of the impact of victimisation, the framing of the survey around conflict, and the lack of insight into the relationship context and motives surrounding the use of violent behaviours. Bluntness concerns the inability of the CTS to usefully distinguish between different degrees of violence; for instance, a push might not even unbalance the 'victim', or conversely—if they are pushed down the stairs—might cause potentially fatal injuries.

Both, however, would be conflated into the same tick-box. Relatedly, the new injuries scale in the CTS-2 is restricted to physical injuries, relying on a partner knowing (and acknowledging) the impacts of their violence on their partner, but also overlooking the widespread impacts of domestic 'abuse' on, *inter alia*, the victim's/survivor's mental health, self-esteem, working life, parenting and subsequent relationships (Abrahams 2007, 2010; Donovan and Hester 2014; Kelly et al. 2014; Kirkwood 1993; Radford and Hester 2006; Stark 2007; Wilcox 2006).

Bluntness also concerns how the results are interpreted. The use of one conflict tactic once in the past 12 months can result in a respondent being categorised as either a victim or a perpetrator of IPVA, despite Straus' own insistence that the tool measures the use of conflict in relationships, not the prevalence of the chronic pattern of abuse that characterises domestic violence and abuse (DVA) as a specific form of IPVA (Straus 1999). This approach to categorising someone as either a victim or a perpetrator is widespread across the quantitative literature, including the LGB and/or T+ IPVA literature (Donovan and Hester 2014). As we examine further in Chap. 3, without further contextualisation, these often very high headline figures can artificially elevate the prevalence of DVA, conflating chronic abuse with any instance of physical, sexual or psychological aggression in an intimate relationship. As outlined in Chap. 1, this issue has been pivotal to Johnson's efforts to develop a more nuanced conceptualisation of IPVA (Johnson 2008), albeit focussing on HC people's experiences to date.

Recruitment to participate in the CTS also raises issues, relying as it does on an appeal to explore conflict:

> No matter how well a couple gets along, there are times when they disagree, get annoyed with the other person, want different things from each other, or just have spats or fights because they are in a bad mood or tired or for some other reason. Couples also have many different ways of trying to settle their differences. This is a list of things that might happen when you have differences. (Straus and Douglas 2004, p. 521)

Such wording raises serious ethical concerns about victims/survivors taking from this preamble that their experiences of victimisation are a normal and legitimate aspect of intimate relationships. Moreover, concentrating on conflict may lead respondents to exclude incidents that are control motivated and without any antecedent conflict (Kimmel 2002).

Finally, the lack of data about the wider relationship dynamics and the context in which 'conflict tactics' are used is a significant limitation. The primary concern which feminist scholars have raised is whether violence and other conflict tactics are used in self-defence (Dobash and Dobash 2004; Loseke and Kurz 2005; Saunders 2002). Straus' response to this criticism is that a measure of self-defence was introduced for the 1985 NFVS, involving asking respondents who 'hit first'. Both the 1985 NFVS and other CTS-based studies, he explains, have found approximately equal rates of initiation by men and women, countering the initial assumption that he had made that women's assaults would be primarily in self-defence (Straus 1999). Yet, studies exploring women's use of violence towards male partners have found that self-defence is not always reactive, and can be anticipatory or in response to threats of violence (Loseke and Kurz 2005; Miller 2001); therefore, simply asking who 'hit first' is too limited. We return to these ideas in Chap. 4, where we unpack our related concept of 'space for reaction'.

Importantly, motives are not asked about, yet this would inform a more complex understanding of how violent and 'abusive' behaviours are used (DeKeseredy and Schwartz 2011; Flynn and Graham 2010; Kimmel 2002). Indeed, since the focus of the CTS is on conflict resolution, the motive is already implied. Researchers using the CTS tend to find that the commonest relationship dynamic is that both partners use conflict tactics, but to call this 'mutual abuse', as they frequently do (Currie 1998; Nicholls and Dutton 2001; Straus 1999), suggests a parity of perpetration and harm that is misleading (Hodes and Mennicke 2019). Apart from the previously mentioned finding that HC women are disproportionately injured by their HC male partners (Archer 2000; Straus 1999, 2005), the lack of nuance resulting from a 'violence is violence' approach is deeply problematic, failing to understand exactly what is happening in relationships where violence and 'abusive' behaviours are used, and subsequently to develop appropriate responses.

Consequently, alternative methods have been sought. For some, these alternatives have remained within the quantitative paradigm, but have

involved developing instruments which seek to better capture the dynamics of power and control and the impacts of victimisation (see Bender
2017). A number of these approaches were discussed in Chap. 1, including attempts to extend Johnson's (2008) typology of IPVA, as well as to
explore whether the violence is unidirectional or bidirectional; and using
cluster analysis to generate expanded typologies of IPV (Frankland and
Brown 2014; Mennicke and Kulkarni 2016; Messinger et al. 2014,
2018). Others, particularly feminist researchers, have favoured qualitative methods, using in-depth interviews with victims/survivors (Abrahams
2007, 2010; Dobash and Dobash 1979; Kirkwood 1993; Ristock 2002;
Wilcox 2006) and perpetrators (Anderson and Umberson 2001; Dobash
et al. 2000; Edin and Nilsson 2014; Hearn 1998). More recently, other
creative qualitative methods have been used to enable victims/survivors
to express themselves, such as arts-based methods, including collage (Bird
2018) and photography (Frohmann 2005).

Mixed-methods research, which enables the triangulation of quantitative data with richer, more contextual qualitative data, has also developed. In an early example, Currie (1998) enabled survey respondents to
add contextualising free-text information about their experiences. This
highlighted differences in (ostensibly HC) men's and women's accounts
of the nature and impacts of violent incidents, thus calling into question
what on the surface appears to be gender symmetry. Gadd and colleagues'
(2003) research investigated the discrepancy between men's self-reported
'domestic abuse' victimisation in the 2000 Scottish Crime Survey and
much lower levels of reporting to the police by male victims of IPVA. They
interviewed 44 men and found that 13 men denied ever experiencing
threats or physical force from a partner (Gadd et al. 2003). As we also
demonstrate with our own data in Chaps. 3 and 4, contextualisation of
quantitative data with qualitative data is vital to avoid assuming that all
violence is equivalent, generating overly simplistic binaries of victim/per-
petrator from quantitative data and/or making simplistic assumptions
about 'mutual abuse'.

Finally, the innovative mixed-methods approach developed for the
Comparing Heterosexual and Same-Sex Abuse in Relationships
(COHSAR) research (Donovan et al. 2006; Donovan and Hester 2014)
is important to note, both for its wider contribution to IPVA research

and as a precursor to the research which this book is based on. The COHSAR research—the most detailed study of DVA in 'same-sex' relationships in the UK to date—involved a detailed questionnaire which sought to surpass the limitations noted above by capturing much more detailed data about the motives and impacts of perpetration and victimisation, respectively, as well as including sexuality-specific forms of DVA such as threatening to out a partner (Hester et al. 2010). The questionnaire was then used to recruit interview participants, enabling a much more extensive exploration of their experiences. The Coral Project adopts many successful aspects of the COHSAR study, while also building on it in order to collect more in-depth, original data about IPVA perpetration.

2.2.3 Sampling and Heteronormative, Cisnormative Assumptions in IPVA Research

Sampling is one of the key differences between research conducted by family violence researchers and feminist scholars. Family violence research is most often based on general population mixed-sex survey samples, both random and non-random. Conversely, feminist research has typically been conducted with smaller, non-random clinical or agency samples of women (e.g. from refuges). There are limitations to each: general survey samples under-represent the most serious and chronic cases of IPVA, because victims of this type of IPVA are less likely to participate (Johnson 2008; Loseke and Kurz 2005), while feminist research over-represents coercive controlling violence (CCV), because many IPVA interventions—refuge provision especially—are restricted to women who are deemed to be at the highest risk and need (Graham-Kevan and Archer 2003; Johnson 2011). Thus, neither strategy provides a comprehensive picture of the prevalence of chronic IPVA. Johnson et al. (2014) also point to the importance of asking about both current and previous relationships. Finally, feminist research has been criticised for only surveying women about their victimisation and not their perpetration (Straus 2005). Thus, whilst large-scale studies such as the EU-wide violence against women survey (FRA 2014) yield oft-cited prevalence figures, the lack of comparable figures for men can serve as a distraction from their important findings.

Critically, the preoccupation with the gender symmetry versus asymmetry debate reinforces the invisibility of LGB and/or T+ people and their relationships. As highlighted in Chap. 1, in almost all mainstream IPVA research, we are seldom told anything about the sexuality and gender identity of participants or the partners they report on, with the assumption being that these samples are cisgender and heterosexual (Baker et al. 2013; Donovan and Barnes 2019). Indeed, whilst some government surveys are now starting to collect and analyse data on sexuality (see Messinger 2011; ONS 2018; Walters et al. 2013), very few academic studies even make explicit that they are investigating HC people or relationships, or explain how they identified and/or excluded (either before data collection or afterwards) participants who were not in heterosexual relationships. This exposes flaws regarding the assumptions made in empirical and theoretical claims about gender (a)symmetry that respondents will be reporting on opposite-sex partners (see Donovan and Barnes 2019 for further discussion and critique).

Thus, for the benefit of both the mainstream and LGBT+ IPVA literature, a different story needs to be told. As Baker et al. (2013) argue, studying IPV in 'same-sex' relationships can offer fresh insights into IPVA more generally. Although their focus on physical violence is rather narrow, Baker et al. (2013) make a compelling argument for moving beyond treating gender as a simple binary variable, and instead probing how gender and other biographical, psychological and social-structural factors shape willingness to use violence, relationship interactions and approaches to conflict resolution. Eliciting and problematising the gender and sexuality of participants, as well as moving beyond assumptions that all intimate relationships are dyadic, is key to developing more complex understandings of IPVA, gender, power and intimacy, which reflect more diverse ways of living out gender, sexuality and intimacies.

Returning to sampling, it has not been possible to identify random samples of LGB and/or T+ people from the general population, due to the absence of an appropriate sampling frame; plus, opportunities to access survivors or perpetrators via agencies are much more limited due to the scarcity of LGBT-inclusive support services and interventions. Consequently, many studies are based on self-selected convenience samples from the general LGB and/or T+ population, which are usually much smaller than studies of the HC population. However, this strategy simultaneously obscures 'true' prevalence by over-representing those who identify with the topic of the questionnaire, whilst also under-representing LGB and/or T+ people who do not engage with LGBT+ social spaces or social media (Barnes and Donovan 2018; Donovan and Hester 2014; Messinger 2014). This in turn reduces the comparability of such samples with the mainstream IPVA literature. Yet, it is important not to overly reify the 'gold-standard' veneer of random samples of the general population. Samples for all voluntary surveys are to some extent self-selected, and it is always important to reflect on how the achieved sample differs from non-responders. We next explain the innovative methodology of the Coral Project.

2.3   The Coral Project's Methodology

The Coral Project was the first mixed-methods study in the UK—and to our knowledge, internationally too—to focus on the use, or perpetration, of violent and 'abusive' behaviours in LGB and/or T+ people's relationships. Our aims were to:

- explore similarities and differences between those who enact 'abusive' behaviours in LGB and/or T+ and HC people's relationships
- collect data from those who have enacted 'abusive' behaviours, as well as from practitioners who provide interventions for predominantly heterosexual male perpetrators
- explore what methods might work best to elicit data to address these aims
- share key findings with key stakeholders to develop best practice guidance for work with those who use 'abusive' behaviours in LGB and/or T+ people's relationships

To achieve these aims, we adopted a mixed-methods study based on the COHSAR research (Donovan and Hester 2014). The methods used to collect this data are outlined next.

2.3.1 The Survey

A UK-wide community survey was conducted to capture as wide a range of relationship experiences as possible, given the difficulties presented in researching a hard-to-reach population about such sensitive issues. Our questionnaire—a modified form of the COHSAR questionnaire—covered the following themes:

- About you—participant demographic data
- Experiences of being out and homo/bi/transphobia (including experiences of reporting to the police and other agencies)
- Intimate relationships—relationship beliefs and expectations, and decision-making and conflict resolution in the participant's current or most recent intimate relationship
- Your partner's behaviour—experiences of physical, emotional, sexual and financial behaviours in the participant's current or most recent intimate relationship and in previous relationships, plus impacts and help-seeking
- Your behaviour—use of physical, emotional, sexual and financial behaviours in the participant's current or most recent intimate relationship and in previous relationships, plus motives, help-seeking, identification of problems with control, anger, trust and jealousy by self and others, and an indicator of 'readiness to change' (Rollnick et al. 1992)

Recruitment to the survey took into account two factors. First, we wished to avoid the aforementioned limitations of research based solely on samples comprising self-defined victims/survivors (or perpetrators). Second, as discussed in Chap. 1, the public story of DVA (Donovan and Hester 2014) inhibits LGB and/or T+ people from recognising their experiences as DVA. Consequently, the Coral Project, mirroring the

COHSAR research (Hester et al. 2010), titled the research 'What do you do when things go wrong in your same-sex, bisexual and/or transgender relationships?'[1]

Importantly, as part of our ethical responsibility towards respondents, the introduction to the questionnaire explained that questions would be asked about sensitive issues such as physical, emotional financial and/or sexual behaviours that may be used in relationships; that their responses would be anonymous[2]; and that they could withdraw by exiting the survey at any time. The survey only invited participation from those aged over 16 years. Finally, the survey included a list of relevant national sources of support. The draft survey was consulted on with our steering group of key practice, policy and academic stakeholders, and was piloted with a group of academic, practitioner and lay critical friends, after which minor changes to question wordings and instructions were made.

The survey was circulated to 200 LGBT+ groups, organisations and venues that had agreed to support and publicise the research. The research team also used social media, especially Twitter, to advertise the survey. As the survey progressed, efforts were made to boost the participation of under-represented groups: people residing outside England; Black, Asian and minority ethnic groups; parents; and older LGB and/or T+ people. Hard copy questionnaires were also distributed to improve accessibility for people without internet access, but returns were negligible. Our initial target of 200 responses was quickly surpassed, and the survey yielded 872 usable responses (from 917 respondents). Given that the pilot study found that the survey took 35–40 minutes to complete, this shows a high level of commitment and generosity on the part of respondents.

Despite its size, no claims to representativeness can be made due to the self-selected nature of the sample. However, the final sample was demographically diverse, as outlined below:

---

[1] We chose the terminology 'same-sex, bisexual and/or transgender relationships' to encompass any relationships where either the respondent or their partner identified as LGB and/or T+. Whilst clunky, our intention was to move beyond the focus in the COHSAR research on same-sex relationships, and to be inclusive of bisexual people with opposite-sex partners and trans+ people who identify as heterosexual. In our work now, we tend to refer to LGB and/or T+ people's relationships, and we also recognise that the terms same-sex and opposite-sex reinforce a cisnormative gender binary.

[2] Respondents were invited to leave their contact details if they were willing to take part in a follow-up interview, but these details were securely stored separately from the rest of their data.

- Respondents were aged 16–70+ years, with the majority (55.5%) being in their 20s and 30s. Young people (only 8.1% were aged 16–19 years) and older people (only 4.4% were aged 60 years or over) were under-represented in the survey.
- A higher proportion of women (including trans women) completed the survey compared with men (including trans men)—54% compared with 41%, respectively—whilst 4% identified as genderqueer or non-binary. Respondents in this latter group were categorised based on free-text descriptions of their gender identity, some of which pointed to a level of fluidity and complexity that a tick-box alone would not capture. Eleven per cent of respondents had ever identified as transgender.
- Overall, 32% of the sample self-defined as gay men, 23.1% as lesbians, 15.3% as gay women and 13.9% as bisexuals. In addition, 5.5% of the sample self-defined as queer, 3.7% as heterosexual and 1.1% as homosexual. Five per cent chose 'other sexual identity', including pansexual, homoflexible, dual/multiple sexual identity and 'do not define/use labels'.
- The vast majority of the sample were white, with 6% identifying as being of mixed ethnicity, Black, Asian, Chinese or belonging to other minority ethnic groups.[3] The majority of respondents were based in England (84.2%), followed by Scotland (8.6%), Wales (5.5%) and Northern Ireland (1.8%).
- Nearly a third of the respondents indicated that they had a disability, including mental health-related disabilities; this is disproportionately higher than the 16% figure for the general UK population (DWP 2014).
- Just over half (52.5%) were employed full-time, just over a fifth (22.2%) were students, and 6.7% were self-employed or employed part-time. Smaller proportions were not in economic activity for various reasons, including long-term illness/impairment, or being unemployed, retired, or a full-time parent or carer.

---

[3] Ethnicity statistics in the UK are devolved, making it difficult to make comparisons with a UK-wide sample. In England and Wales, people in Black, Asian, mixed or other minority ethnic groups accounted for 14% of the population in the 2011 census (ONS 2012). However, the corresponding figures from the 2011 censuses in Scotland and Northern Ireland are just 4% and 1.8%, respectively (Northern Ireland Statistics and Research Agency 2012; Scottish Government 2015).

- Thirteen per cent of respondents were parents.
- As is often the case in research with LGB and/or T+ people (Hartman 2011; Meezan and Martin 2003), respondents were disproportionately well educated, with a third having an undergraduate degree and a further quarter having a postgraduate degree as their highest qualification.
- Educational attainment did not, however, correspond to having a high income. Just over half (51.6%) of the respondents reported a household income of less than £33,000. The largest group reported a household income of between £12,000 and £22,999 (19.4%), which is well below the average income in the UK, which at the time of data collection was £27,000 (ONS 2013).
- Those who identified as genderqueer/non-binary gender were clustered in the lowest income brackets. This may be because these respondents were younger and/or less likely to be in cohabiting relationships. It might also reflect economic disadvantage and social exclusion as a consequence of transphobia and prejudice towards those who do not conform to the gender binary, and also the much higher reporting of disabilities (45.9%), to give an example of the importance of developing an intersectional analysis.

The data was analysed using the statistical analysis software IBM SPSS. This enabled production of descriptive statistics as well as more complex analyses which examined the relationships between two or more variables. Extensive recoding took place in order to explore and test relationships which were relevant to Johnson's (2008) typology of IPVA; for example, relationships between controlling attitudes, dominance in relationships and use of 'abusive' behaviours, and relationships between experience of 'abusive' behaviours and reported impacts.

2.3.2 Follow-Up Interviews

The interviews incorporated semi-structured elements to ensure comparability, whilst also including more narrative, unstructured elements, such as inviting participants to share their coming out story and talk us through their relationship history. Interviews lasted between one and three hours, with most lasting one and a half to two hours. The interview sample was purposively constructed by using the survey as a filter to identify interview participants who appeared from their responses to potentially be perpetrators of IPVA. In order to be selected for interview, participants:

- had expressed willingness to take part in an interview and given their contact details (approximately one-third of the 872 survey respondents)
- were aged 18 years or over
- had self-reported using at least one of the 'abusive' behaviours (but may also have reported being victimised)
- were no longer in a relationship where they were using or experiencing 'abusive' behaviours
- had recognised that their behaviour was a problem and/or taken steps to change their behaviour

Whilst these stipulations restricted the scope of the sample, they were considered essential to minimise risk to the participants and the researchers. The Coral Project adopted an ethical approach intended to protect both participants and researchers in the field. Interviews took place in private rooms within a public venue (e.g. library, community centre), and safety protocols included the interviewer checking in with the research administrator at set intervals. The information sheet provided to all participants before an interview made clear that should they disclose any information likely to raise concerns (such as a child or adult being at current or imminent risk of harm), this would need to be reported to the appropriate agencies. Fortunately, no such concerns were raised.

Our commitment to an 'ethics of care' (Burgess-Proctor 2015; Edwards and Mauthner 2002) prioritised the well-being of participants over the fulfilment of research objectives. Some participants found recalling their experiences distressing, and where this was the case, participants were offered the opportunity to take a break and reconsider their continued involvement. Crucially, securing informed consent is not a one-off, tick-box event, but is rather ongoing throughout the research process (Miller and Bell 2002). Participants were advised that they could withdraw their data after participating in the interview by contacting the researcher. A small number of participants made contact, either shortly after the interview or after reviewing their transcript, to request that certain parts of their transcript be either corrected or redacted. All participants were given an aftercare sheet which listed national organisations and helplines and relevant support services in their local area.

Whilst no claims to representativeness can be made, the demographic profile of the interview sample was comparable to the survey sample, and was diverse in terms of sexuality and gender identity. The interview sample comprised 17 men (including one trans man), 15 of whom identified as gay, one bi and one pansexual; and 19 women (including two trans women), 12 of whom identified as lesbian, one as a gay woman, three as bisexual, two as queer and/or pansexual, and one as asexual. Interview participants ranged from 20 to 68 years old. All but three participants identified as white; the remaining three identified as Chinese, mixed ethnicity or mixed heritage.

Interviews with participants focussed on their coming out story in terms of both their sexuality and their gender identity, as appropriate; their relationship history; their perceptions about how they behaved in relationships in relation to particular aspects of intimate life—for example, dealing with conflict and decision-making; their views about how LGB and/or T+ people's relationships compared with heterosexual people's relationships; any relationship help-seeking they had engaged in, and its utility; and what help they would like to see become available. Three pilot interviews were conducted, giving the opportunity to reflect on how well the interview guide was working and to make minor modifications.

A distinctive feature of our interview design was the use of a vignette or scenario about potentially 'abusive' behaviour in a relationship. Four gender-neutral vignettes were developed to explore interview participants' perceptions of physically, emotionally, sexually and financially 'abusive' behaviours, respectively. Vignettes were not used in all interviews due to time constraints, but where they were, the chosen vignette was tailored strategically to the participant's survey responses in order to open up discussion of relevant relationship experiences. This was effective, since it facilitated a segue, initiated sometimes by the interviewer but also by participants, away from the hypothetical scenario and into reflection upon comparable personal experiences—or sometimes the absence thereof. This is illustrated by Colin, a white, cisgender, gay man in his mid-30s, for whom discussion of the vignette led to a disclosure about his own use of physical violence:

Colin:　　　　　[Regarding the vignette] I think up to that point, before kind of the physical restraint, I think it would just be kind of seen as sort of a lover's tiff kind of thing, but once it goes beyond that, then that's when it becomes a little bit more serious.

Interviewer:　*And have you ever been in a situation that's similar to that?*

Colin:　　　　　Yes. I have.

Interviewer:　*So would you talk through what happened in that situation?*

Colin:　　　　　Yeah. I mean it happened quite a few times, to be perfectly honest, with my ex, from both sides. We both kind of used physical restraint towards each other and even physical violence, whereby I would say the majority of the time it will probably be more me that was the physical aggressor, um rather than my ex.

This way into talking about the enactment of violence and 'abusive' behaviours may benefit from being less confrontational than starting out cold with a question such as 'have you ever been physically violent towards a partner?'

All interviews were transcribed, and the analysis involved two phases. The first—which is most pertinent to this book—involved keeping the transcripts whole and reading them as life histories focussed around participants' experiences of intimate relationships. Throughout this immersive reading process, we looked for predefined codes which derived from Johnson's (2008) typology of IPVA whilst also looking for accounts which raised different issues and/or which did not easily fit into Johnson's typology. Both authors read each transcript, and we independently categorised each account and then discussed how we had made sense of them, subsequently reaching a final decision. Keeping the transcripts whole rather than breaking them down into themes was important for this element, in order not to lose a sense of the context and dynamics of the relationship, particularly in relation to how any 'abusive' behaviours were used or experienced. The second phase of the analysis, which is ongoing, involves a thematic analysis of the transcripts, making use of the qualitative software package NVivo to code and organise the data. This phase incorporates a much broader range of themes than the concerns of this book, including relationship expectations, attitudes towards conflict in relationships, and the adequacy of existing role models and support for LGB and/or T+ people's intimate relationships.

2.4   Insights from Triangulating Survey and Interview Data

Through triangulating the survey and interview data, it became apparent that how participants interpreted terms in the survey differed from how we as researchers had interpreted and intended them (Ackerman 2016). Without this qualitative triangulation, we would have been less aware of the subjectivity of interpretation of language and terminology in surveys. It is important to note that this applied to some of the more overtly physically violent behaviours too and is not therefore an issue with arguably more ambiguous behaviours. Paul, a white, cisgender, gay man with a disability, and in his 50s at the time of the interview, illustrates one type of difference in interpretation. He had completed the survey indicating that he had both experienced and enacted several types of physical violence. On interview, it transpired that these behaviours had been part of consensual bondage, discipline, sadism and masochism (BDSM) relationships.

In another example, Jack, another cisgender white gay man in his mid-40s, ticked in the survey that he had threatened to kill an (ex-)partner. Whilst this initially appears to be a straightforward case of aggressive violence/threats from somebody who is unequivocally a perpetrator, Jack's interview account shows how even threats to kill need to be understood in context. Jack recalled a relationship that he had had when he was in his mid-20s with Donald, a man who was nearly 30 years his senior. Donald invited Jack to move some distance to live with him, and became controlling and financially abusive:

[H]e had so much control over me that I found myself going up to bank machines at midnight on, on pay day, and taking hundreds of pounds out and handing it to him at the machine, just because he […] needed the money, and because I just didn't know how to deal with this […] it's so difficult to explain, it just gradually worked its way to a position where I was completely under his spell.

When Jack showed signs of resisting the control, Donald threatened to out him to schools where Jack had been looking to become a teacher. Then, when Jack told Donald that he was going to leave, Donald became physically violent. At this point, Jack left the relationship and returned to his family home. However, Donald continued his post-separation abuse, telephoning him and 'screaming abuse down the phone'. Jack was not out to his family at the time and could not explain what was happening to them. This continued for 14 months until Jack created a space for reaction. His response can only be understood in the context of Jack's national and religious identity. He was from a Catholic area in Northern Ireland, and this experience took place during what the UK government called 'the Troubles', when paramilitary groups from both Catholic and Protestant communities engaged in military-like campaigns to achieve their political ends of, respectively, ending and defending British rule in Northern Ireland:

It's not funny but it's funny. I threatened him with the IRA [Irish Republican Army] [laughs] at the time. I says, 'I come from a Catholic town, and I have contacts, and if you set foot [here] I'll have you shot', and I never heard from him again, and that was it. But I mean, I didn't know anybody, it was just a threat, it was an empty threat, but he […] wasn't going to take the chance.

This threat, made out of desperation to end Donald's persistent coercive and controlling pursuit of Jack, can be understood as Jack creating a space for reaction with an act of non-physical violent resistance to deter Donald from contacting him again. It worked; Jack never heard from Donald again and was able to restart his life. Jack's account is a vivid illustration of the need to capture context and the very different understandings that this gives us compared to relying on the quantitative data alone.

Some might question whether inconsistencies between the survey and interview data point to dishonesty or selectivity in either the survey or the interview. There may be various explanations for the differences between the two subsets of data. As sociologists, we recognise that how people make sense of experiences is socially constructed and thus shaped by external influences, which over time can lead to people reinterpreting experiences or situations (Presser 2009; Riessman 2008). Certainly, for victims/survivors of DVA it can take time to realise or acknowledge that they are being abused; this may not occur until after the relationship has ended, if at all (Donovan and Hester 2010; Francis et al. 2017). Memory and selectivity—especially when mediated by shame, embarrassment and/or guilt—also shape what is shared with researchers, and how (Barnes 2013; Riessman 2008). However, our position is that there is no one 'truth' about a relationship, but that what is remembered, even if selective, usefully reveals something about how individuals make sense of the different ways in which IPVA is enacted.

Additionally, in contrast to concerns raised in some research with heterosexual male perpetrators (Hearn 1998; Kelly and Westmarland 2016), we did not see evidence of interview participants exaggerating their victimisation or, in the main, downplaying their own behaviour. On the contrary, interview participants were often reflective, careful and measured when giving their accounts, as we shall illustrate in Chap. 4. However, it is important to reiterate that interview participants were drawn from a convenience sample of the general LGB and/or T+ population, and not a clinical sample of DVA perpetrators. Further, participants who took part in the interviews were motivated to do so because of their own experiences not just of IPVA but also of seeking help, and/or they were active in their LGB and/or T+ communities locally and nationally and were very often 'givers' to the community. That they were willing to provide sometimes quite painful accounts of their own use of violence is testament to their commitment to improving things in general for LGB and/or T+ people.

2.5   Summary

This chapter has demonstrated that whilst IPVA research, at least in relation to HC people's relationships, has been developing for almost half a century, significant questions and concerns continue to surround the methodologies and measures that are used. This has critical implications for the reliability and validity of the data that different approaches yield. The long-running debate about the gender symmetry or asymmetry of IPVA has taken up a vast amount of time which could be used to develop more holistic and meaningful understandings of IPVA. As has been discussed, the problems of this ongoing argument are first that it reifies physical, and sometimes sexual, violence; second, it is based on attempts to compare the incomparable—different methodologies, different samples, different measures of IPVA, different time frames; and third, it restricts itself to a rigid binaried notion of gender, whilst assuming that all respondents will be in, or reporting on, a heterosexual relationship.

Whilst the existence of LGBT+ IPVA is sometimes used to argue that the gender asymmetrical conceptualisation of IPVA is incorrect, LGBT+ IPVA has otherwise been largely ignored by family violence scholars and feminist scholars alike. Thus, the LGBT+ IPVA literature is at an earlier stage of development. As LGBT+ IPVA researchers, we have not experienced the luxury of being able to conduct large-scale surveys with randomly selected representative samples, although opportunities are now starting to open up with the inclusion of questions about sexuality and gender identity in some national representative surveys (Messinger 2011; ONS 2018; Walters et al. 2013). On the one hand, this means that LGBT+ IPVA research carries numerous caveats and cautions because of its typically smaller self-selecting samples. On the other hand, it frees researchers up—indeed, mandates researchers—to explore and implement more innovative and creative approaches to secure suitable samples from what could be described as hidden or hard-to-reach populations.

However, as LGBT+ IPVA research develops, it is important that it does not replicate some of the flaws that are deeply embedded in the mainstream IPVA literature—not least, a focus on counting without developing deeper understanding. DVA relationships are enormously complex and diverse in how they develop, their dynamics and their consequences. Our methodological approaches therefore need to be complex and nuanced if we hope to capture the different dimensions of IPVA.

Our Coral Project methodology tested one such approach to collecting richer and more nuanced data about IPVA in LGB and/or T+ people's relationships. When we started out on this research, we did not know whether we could develop a survey instrument through which respondents would disclose the acts of violence and 'abuse' that they had enacted in their current and previous relationships. Yet, we were successful in locating a sample of LGB and/or T+ people who had used 'abusive' behaviours in their relationships for a wide range of reasons—including some who had also experienced considerable victimisation—and who were willing to share these with us in the survey, and in some cases in follow-up interviews. In the chapters that follow, we share our findings and how they enable us to tell different stories about IPVA.

References

Abrahams, H. (2007). *Supporting women after domestic violence: Loss, trauma and recovery*. London: Jessica Kingsley Press.

Abrahams, H. (2010). *Rebuilding lives after domestic violence: Understanding long-term outcomes*. London: Jessica Kingsley Press.

Acker, J., Barry, K., & Esseveld, J. (1983). Objectivity and truth: Problems in doing feminist research. *Women's Studies International Forum, 6*(4), 423–435.

Ackerman, J. M. (2016). Over-reporting intimate partner violence in Australian survey research. *British Journal of Criminology, 56*(4), 646–667.

Anderson, K. L., & Umberson, D. (2001). Gendering violence: Masculinity and power in men's accounts of domestic violence. *Gender and Society, 15*(3), 358–380.

Archer, J. (2000). Sex differences in aggression between heterosexual partners: A meta-analytic review. *Psychological Bulletin, 126*, 651–680.

Archer, J. (2002). Sex differences in physically aggressive acts between heterosexual partners: A meta-analytic review. *Aggression and Violent Behavior, 7*(4), 313–351.

Baker, N. L., Buick, J. D., Kim, S. R., Moniz, S., & Nava, K. L. (2013). Lessons from examining same-sex intimate partner violence. *Sex Roles: A Journal of Research, 69*(3–4), 182–192.

Barnes, R. (2013). 'I'm over it': Survivor narratives after woman-to-woman partner abuse. *Partner Abuse, 4*(3), 380–398.

Barnes, R., & Donovan, C. (2018). Domestic violence in lesbian, gay, bisexual and/or transgender relationships. In N. Lombard (Ed.), *Gender and violence research companion* (pp. 67–81). London: Routledge.

Bender, A. K. (2017). Ethics, methods and measures in intimate partner violence research: The current state of the field. *Violence Against Women, 23*(11), 1382–1413.

Bird, J. (2018). Art therapy, arts-based research and transitional stories of domestic violence and abuse. *International Journal of Art Therapy, 23*(1), 14–24.

Burgess-Proctor, A. (2015). Methodological and ethical issues in feminist research with abused women: Reflections on participants' vulnerability and empowerment. *Women's Studies International Forum, 48*, 124–134.

Currie, D. H. (1998). Violent men or violent women? Whose definition counts? In R. K. Bergen (Ed.), *Issues in intimate violence* (pp. 97–111). London: Sage.

DeKeseredy, W. S., & Schwartz, M. D. (2011). Theoretical and definitional issues in violence against women. In C. M. Renzetti, J. L. Edelson, & R. K. Bergen (Eds.), *Sourcebook on violence against women* (2nd ed., pp. 3–22). London: Sage.

Department for Work and Pensions (DWP). (2014). *Disability facts and figures.* Retrieved September 9, 2019, from https://www.gov.uk/government/publications/disability-facts-and-figures/disability-facts-and-figures

Dobash, R. E., & Dobash, R. P. (1979). *Violence against wives: A case against the patriarchy.* New York: Free Press.

Dobash, R. E., Dobash, R. P., Cavanagh, K., & Lewis, R. (2000). *Changing violent men.* London: Sage.

Dobash, R. P., & Dobash, R. E. (2004). Women's violence to men in intimate relationships: Working on a puzzle. *British Journal of Criminology, 44*(3), 324–349.

Dobash, R. P., Dobash, R. E., Wilson, M., & Daly, M. (1992). The myth of sexual symmetry in marital violence. *Social Problems, 39*(1), 71–91.

Donovan, C., & Barnes, R. (2019, July 26). Re-tangling the concept of coercive control: A view from the margins and a response to Walby and Towers (2018). *Criminology and Criminal Justice.* https://doi.org/10.1177/1748895819864622

Donovan, C., & Hester, M. (2010). 'I hate the word "victim"': An exploration of recognition of domestic violence in same sex relationships. *Social Policy and Society, 9*(2), 279–289.

Donovan, C., & Hester, M. (2014). *Domestic violence and sexuality: What's love got to do with it?* Bristol: Policy Press.

Donovan, C., Hester, M., Holmes, J., & McCarry, M. (2006). *Comparing domestic abuse in same sex and heterosexual relationships: Initial report from a study funded by the Economic & Social Research Council.* Sunderland and Bristol: University of Sunderland and University of Bristol. Retrieved March 30, 2019, from http://www.equation.org.uk/wp-content/uploads/2012/12/Comparing-Domestic-Abuse-in-Same-Sex-and-Heterosexual-relationships.pdf

Edin, K., & Nilsson, B. (2014). Men's violence: Narratives of men attending anti-violence programmes in Sweden. *Women's Studies International Forum, 46*, 96–106.

Edwards, R., & Mauthner, M. (2002). Ethics and feminist research: Theory and practice. In M. Mauthner, M. Birch, J. Jessop, & T. Miller (Eds.), *Ethics in qualitative research* (pp. 14–31). London: Sage.

Flynn, A., & Graham, K. (2010). 'Why did it happen?': A review and conceptual framework for research on perpetrators' and victims' explanations for intimate partner violence. *Aggression and Violent Behavior, 15*, 239–251.

Francis, L., Loxton, D., & James, C. (2017). The culture of pretence: A hidden barrier to recognising, disclosing and ending domestic violence. *Journal of Clinical Nursing, 26*(15/16), 2202–2214.

Frankland, A., & Brown, J. (2014). Coercive control in same-sex intimate partner violence. *Journal of Family Violence, 29*(1), 15–22.

Frohmann, L. (2005). The framing safety project: Photographs and narratives by battered women. *Violence Against Women, 11*(11), 1396–1419.

Fundamental Rights Agency (FRA). (2014). *Violence against women: An EU-wide survey: Main results.* Vienna: European Union Agency for Fundamental Rights.

Gadd, D., Farrall, S., Dallimore, D., & Lombard, L. (2003). Equal victims or the usual suspects? Making sense of domestic abuse against men. *International Review of Victimology, 10*, 95–116.

Gavey, N. (1999). 'I wasn't raped, but…': Revisiting definitional problems in sexual victimization. In S. Lamb (Ed.), *New versions of victims: Feminists struggle with the concept* (pp. 57–81). London: New York University Press.

Graham-Kevan, N., & Archer, J. (2003). Intimate terrorism and common couple violence: A test of Johnson's predictions in four British samples. *Journal of Interpersonal Violence, 18*(11), 1247–1270.

Hartman, J. (2011). Finding a needle in a haystack: Methods for sampling in the bisexual community. *Journal of Bisexuality, 11*(1), 64–74.

Hearn, J. (1998). *The violences of men: How men talk about and how agencies respond to men's violence to women.* London: Sage.

Hester, M., Donovan, C., & Fahmy, E. (2010). Feminist epistemology and the politics of method: Surveying same sex domestic violence. *International Journal of Social Research Methodology, 13*(3), 251–263.

Hodes, C., & Mennicke, A. (2019). Is it conflict or abuse? A practice note for furthering differential assessment and response. *Journal of Clinical Social Work, 47*(2), 176–184.

Jaquier, V., Johnson, H., & Fisher, B. S. (2010). Research methods, measures, and ethics. In C. M. Renzetti, J. L. Edelson, & R. K. Bergen (Eds.), *Sourcebook on violence against women* (2nd ed., pp. 23–48). London: Sage.

Johnson, M. P. (2008). *A typology of domestic violence: Intimate terrorism, violent resistance, and situational couple violence.* Boston: Northeastern University Press.

Johnson, M. P. (2011). Gender and types of intimate partner violence: A response to an anti-feminist literature review. *Aggression and Violent Behavior, 16*(4), 289–296.

Johnson, M. P., Leone, J. M., & Xu, Y. (2014). Intimate terrorism and situational couple violence in general surveys: Ex-spouses required. *Violence Against Women, 20*(2), 186–207.

Karakurt, G., & Silver, K. E. (2013). Emotional abuse in intimate relationships: The role of gender and age. *Violence & Victims, 28*(5), 804–821.

Kelly, L., Sharp, N., & Klein, R. (2014). *Finding the costs of freedom: How women and children rebuild their lives after domestic violence.* London: Solace Women's Aid.

Kelly, L., & Westmarland, N. (2016). Naming and defining 'domestic violence': Lessons from research with violent men. *Feminist Review, 112*(1), 113–127.

Kimmel, M. S. (2002). 'Gender symmetry' in domestic violence: A substantive and methodological research review. *Violence Against Women, 8*(11), 1332–1363.

Kirkwood, C. (1993). *Leaving abusive partners: From the scars of survival to the wisdom for change.* London: Sage.

Loseke, D. R., & Kurz, D. (2005). Men's violence toward women is the serious social problem. In D. R. Loseke, R. J. Gelles, & M. M. Cavanuagh (Eds.), *Current controversies in family violence* (2nd ed., pp. 79–95). London: Sage.

Meezan, J. E., & Martin, J. I. (2003). Exploring current themes in research on gay, lesbian, bisexual and transgender populations. *Journal of Gay & Lesbian Social Services, 15*(1/2), 1–14.

Mennicke, A., & Kulkarni, S. (2016). Understanding gender symmetry within an expanded partner violence typology. *Journal of Family Violence, 31*, 1013–1018.

Messinger, A. M. (2011). Invisible victims: Same-sex IPV in the national violence against women survey. *Journal of Interpersonal Violence, 26*(11), 2228–2243.

Messinger, A. M. (2014). Marking 35 years of research on same-sex intimate partner violence: Lessons and new directions. In D. Peterson & V. Panfil (Eds.), *Handbook of LGBT communities, crime, and justice* (pp. 65–85). New York: Springer.

Messinger, A. M., Fry, D. A., Rickert, V. I., Catallozzi, M., & Davidson, L. L. (2014). Extending Johnson's intimate partner violence typology: Lessons from an adolescent sample. *Violence Against Women, 20*(8), 948–971.

Messinger, A. M., Sessarego, S. N., Edwards, K. M., & Banyard, V. L. (2018). Bidirectional IPV among adolescent sexual minorities. *Journal of Interpersonal Violence*. https://doi.org/10.1177/0886260518807218

Miller, S. L. (2001). The paradox of women arrested for domestic violence: Criminal justice professionals and service providers respond. *Violence Against Women, 7*(12), 1339–1376.

Miller, T., & Bell, L. (2002). Consenting to what? Issues of access, gate-keeping and informed consent. In M. Mauthner, M. Birch, J. Jessop, & T. Miller (Eds.), *Ethics in qualitative research* (pp. 53–69). London: Sage.

Myhill, A. (2017). Measuring domestic violence: Context is everything. *Journal of Gender-Based Violence, 1*, 33–44.

Myhill, A., & Kelly, L. (2019, July 11). Counting with understanding? What is at stake in debates on researching domestic violence. *Criminology & Criminal Justice*. https://doi.org/10.1177/1748895819863098

Nicholls, T. L., & Dutton, D. G. (2001). Abuse committed by women against male intimates. *Journal of Couples Therapy, 10*(1), 41–57.

Northern Ireland Statistics and Research Agency. (2012). *Census 2011: Key statistics for Northern Ireland*. Belfast: Department of Finance and Personnel.

Office for National Statistics (ONS). (2012). *Ethnicity and national identity in England and Wales: 2011*. London: ONS.

Office for National Statistics (ONS). (2013). *Annual survey of hours and earnings: 2013 provisional results*. London: ONS.

Office for National Statistics (ONS). (2018). *Women most at risk of experiencing partner abuse in England and Wales: Years ending March 2015 to 2017.* London: ONS.

Presser, L. (2009). The narratives of offenders. *Theoretical Criminology, 13*(2), 177–200.

Radford, L., & Hester, M. (2006). *Mothering through domestic violence.* London: Jessica Kingsley Press.

Riessman, C. K. (2008). *Narrative methods for the human sciences.* London: Sage.

Ristock, J. (2002). *No more secrets: Violence in lesbian relationships.* London and New York: Routledge.

Rollnick, S., Heather, N., Gold, R., & Hall, W. (1992). Development of a short 'readiness to change' questionnaire for use in brief, opportunistic interventions among excessive drinkers. *British Journal of Addiction, 87*(5), 743–754.

Ruel, E., Wagner, W. E., III, & Gillespie, B. J. (2016). *The practice of survey research: Theory and applications.* Thousand Oaks, CA: Sage.

Saunders, D. G. (2002). Are physical assaults by wives and girlfriends a major social problem? A review of the literature. *Violence Against Women, 8*(12), 1424–1448.

Scottish Government. (2015). *Analysis of equality results from the 2011 Census—Part 2.* Edinburgh: Scottish Government.

Stark, E. (2007). *Coercive control: How men entrap women in personal life.* Oxford: Oxford University Press.

Straus, M. A. (1979). Measuring intrafamily conflict and violence: The Conflict Tactics (CT) Scales. *Journal of Marriage and Family, 41*(1), 75–88.

Straus, M. A. (1999). The controversy over domestic violence by women: A methodological, theoretical, and sociology of science analysis. In X. B. Arriaga & S. Oskamp (Eds.), *Violence in intimate relationships* (pp. 17–44). London: Sage.

Straus, M. A. (2004). Prevalence of violence against dating partners by male and female university students worldwide. *Violence Against Women, 10*(7), 790–811.

Straus, M. A. (2005). Women's violence toward men is a serious social problem. In D. R. Loseke, R. J. Gelles, & M. N. Cavanaugh (Eds.), *Current controversies in family violence* (2nd ed., pp. 55–77). London: Sage.

Straus, M. A., & Douglas, E. M. (2004). A short form of the revised Conflict Tactics Scales, and typologies for severity and mutuality. *Violence and Victims, 19*(5), 507–521.

Straus, M. A., Hamby, S. L., Boney-McCoy, S., & Sugarman, D. B. (1996). The revised Conflict Tactics Scales (CTS2): Development and preliminary psychometric data. *Journal of Family Issues, 17*(3), 283–316.

Walby, S., & Myhill, A. (2001). New survey methodologies in researching violence against women. *British Journal of Criminology, 41*(3), 502–522.

Walby, S., & Towers, J. (2018). Untangling the concept of coercive control: Theorizing domestic violent crime. *Criminology and Criminal Justice, 18*(1), 7–28.

Walters, M. L., Chen, J., & Breiding, M. J. (2013). *The National Intimate Partner and Sexual Violence Survey (NISVS): 2010 findings on victimization by sexual orientation*. Atlanta: National Center for Injury Prevention and Control, Centers for Disease Control and Prevention.

Wilcox, P. (2006). *Surviving domestic violence: Gender, poverty and agency*. Basingstoke: Palgrave Macmillan.

3

Queering Quantitative Stories of Intimate Partner Violence and Abuse

Abstract Chapter 3 presents the findings from the Coral Project survey about LGB and/or T+ people's experience and use of violence and 'abusive' behaviours. The approach taken deviates from more conventional approaches to reporting on quantitative data, aiming instead to queer the dominant quantitative narrative in intimate partner violence and abuse (IPVA) research. We examine our 'headline' prevalence figures and gender, sexuality and age differences therein. We subsequently explore the heterogeneity of 'perpetrators' of IPVA by comparing subgroups of high/low perpetration and high/low victimisation, leading us to trouble the victim/perpetrator binary. We apply Johnson's typology of IPVA to this analysis and we endeavour to overcome the limitations of much previous IPVA research that is incident-based and typically fails to capture coercive control and the wider relationship context. Our highly original data about the use of violence and 'abusive' behaviours in LGB and/or T+ people's relationships includes findings concerning the reported motives of those who have enacted violence and 'abusive' behaviours, the impacts of victimisation, and the power and control dynamics of respondents' intimate relationships. Throughout, we acknowledge that whilst our survey data offers unique insights, it is not possible to rely solely on it to

© The Author(s) 2020
C. Donovan, R. Barnes, *Queering Narratives of Domestic Violence and Abuse*, Palgrave Studies in Victims and Victimology, https://doi.org/10.1007/978-3-030-35403-9_3

understand how violence, abuse and power operate in people's intimate relationships.

Keywords Coercive control • Domestic violence and abuse • Intimate partner violence and abuse • Lesbian, gay, bisexual and/or transgender • Intersectionality • Measuring intimate partner violence and abuse • Mutual abuse • Perpetrators • Quantitative • Queering • Typologies of domestic violence and abuse • Victims/survivors

3.1 Introduction

In this chapter, we use our survey data from the Coral Project (n = 872) to queer the dominant quantitative narrative in intimate partner violence and abuse (IPVA) research. This queering has two dimensions: the first is to draw LGB and/or T+ people's experiences into the centre of a narrative which has largely excluded them. We do this by presenting highly original empirical data about LGB and/or T+ people's relationship experiences, particularly regarding their use of violence and 'abusive' behaviours. The second dimension of queering goes beyond simply bringing LGB and/or T+ people into existing narratives (Ball 2016); rather, it is to be more radical in disrupting, troubling and seeking to transform existing ways of measuring and conceptualising IPVA.

We first unpack our headline prevalence figures, arguing that a nuanced approach that handles these figures very carefully is needed. Within this section we explore patterns in relation to gender, sexuality and age, highlighting the considerably higher prevalence of IPVA amongst trans+ and bisexual respondents. Next, we reveal the heterogeneity of 'perpetrators' of IPVA and the limitations of the victim/perpetrator binary by comparing subgroups categorised as high perpetration and low perpetration. Although we did not set out to design a study that would test Johnson's (2008) typology of IPVA (or other expanded typologies that have been devised parallel to or since the Coral Project, as discussed in Chap. 1) with our sample, we explore different ways of analysing the data that resonate with this typology. This analysis is grounded in the recognition that existing tools for measuring IPVA are incident-based and typically fail to capture coercive control and the wider relationship context (Frankland and Brown 2014; Hester et al. 2017; Hodes and Mennicke 2019; Myhill and Kelly 2019). We endeavour to address this by examining the reported motives of those who have enacted violence and 'abusive' behaviours, the impacts of victimisation, and the power and control dynamics of respondents' intimate relationships. Throughout, we grapple with the tensions between making effective use of our survey data, which is highly original and innovative, and recognising the limitations of relying on quantitative data alone to make sense of how violence, abuse and power operate in intimate relationships.

3.2 Queering 'Headline' Prevalence Figures (1): Bringing LGB and/or T+ People in

Arriving at a reliable headline prevalence figure has been the goal of much previous LGBT+ IPVA research. In Sects. 3.2 and 3.3 we unpack our own headline prevalence figures for the experience and enactment of violence and 'abusive' behaviours, whilst casting doubt on how meaningful these figures actually are.

Other studies which measure prevalence focus on varying time frames ranging from the last 6 to 12 months, to lifetime prevalence (Badenes-Ribera et al. 2016; Finneran and Stephenson 2012). As noted in Chap. 1, specific time periods have the limitation of potentially capturing more than one intimate relationship. We have sought to overcome this through our first and main measure of prevalence which asks about the last 12 months of a specific (their current or most recent) relationship context. Our prevalence figures measure experience of (victimisation) and enactment of (perpetration) 69–70 different physically, emotionally, sexually and financially violent and 'abusive' behaviours. The measures used were:

1. one or more behaviours reported in the last 12 months of the respondent's current or most recent intimate relationship;
2. one or more behaviours reported in any other same-sex, bisexual and/or transgender relationship since the age of 16; and

Table 3.1 Headline prevalence figures for victimisation

Form of abuse	Percentage of respondents who have experienced any behaviour in the *last 12 months of their current/most recent relationship* (valid *n*)	Percentage of respondents who have experienced any behaviour *in any other same-sex/bi/trans relationship* (valid *n*)
Emotional	54.9 (537)	65.0 (323)
Financial	27.8 (724)	35.1 (542)
Physical	21.0 (675)	39.7 (486)
Sexual	35.2 (687)	48.7 (439)
Combined[a]	64.3 (441)	70.0 (223)

[a]The 'combined abuse' measure includes all of the separate physical, emotional, sexual and financial 'abusive' behaviours. Items with particularly high rates of missing data were removed to maximise the valid sample size, namely, items which related to transitioning and children/parenting. Subsequently, this variable uses data from 64 victimisation items and 65 perpetration items (see Appendix A). The sample sizes for each set of scales (emotional, physical etc.) is typically much lower than the overall sample size (*n* = 872) because of missing data across the items in each scale

3. one or more behaviours reported in any previous heterosexual relationship since the age of 16. (Limited data was collected about previous heterosexual relationships, therefore we have excluded it from our analysis.)

Table 3.1 presents the prevalence figures for victimisation, showing the results for each category of abuse, and then the combined headline prevalence figure which encompasses all four categories of IPVA. The majority of the sample reported experiencing any victimisation in their current/most recent relationship (64.3%) and in any other previous same-sex, bisexual and/or trans relationship (70.0%).

Consistent with previous research (Badenes-Ribera et al. 2016; Donovan and Hester 2014; Finneran and Stephenson 2012; Messinger 2011), emotional behaviours were most commonly reported. Across both current/most recent and previous same-sex, bisexual and/or trans relationships, the second most common form was sexual abuse. However, behaviours from all categories were widely reported in the last 12 months of respondents' current or most recent relationship, as well as across any of their other same-sex, bisexual and/or trans relationships since the age of 16.

Table 3.2 Headline prevalence figures for perpetration

Form of abuse	Percentage of respondents who have used any behaviour in the *last 12 months of their current/ most recent relationship* (valid *n*)	Percentage of respondents who have used any behaviour *in any other same-sex/bi/trans relationship* (valid *n*)
Emotional	44.9 (583)	44.3 (409)
Financial	20.1 (726)	19.3 (596)
Physical	16.0 (667)	26.7 (544)
Sexual	16.1 (684)	20.0 (544)
Combined	55.4 (484)	48.2 (326)

Rates of reported perpetration were lower than for victimisation, but substantial proportions of respondents reported enacting a range of IPVA behaviours (see Table 3.2).

As Table 3.2 shows, more than half of the respondents reported enacting at least one violent and/or 'abusive' behaviour in the last 12 months of their current or most recent relationship (55.4%). Whilst much of this is accounted for by the use of emotional behaviours, 16% of the sample reported using at least one physical and sexual behaviour, respectively. The overall pattern was similar for previous same-sex, bisexual and/or trans relationships, although the combined abuse prevalence for perpetration is—perhaps counter-intuitively—lower for respondents' span of previous relationships since the age of 16 (48.2%) than it was for the 12-month time frame. This may be reflective of respondents being drawn to participate in the survey because of difficulties in their current or most recent relationship and/or not having much experience of previous relationships, or it could reflect respondents' long-term recall of perpetration behaviours being more limited than their recall of victimisation behaviours. The majority of previous perpetration is accounted for by the disclosure of emotional behaviours, although more than one in four respondents (26.7%) reported having used at least one physical behaviour in a previous same-sex, bisexual and/or trans relationship.

3.2.1 Gender, Sexuality and Age Patterns

Headline prevalence figures were also analysed across gender, sexuality and age. This is important as part of the intersectional approach which we outlined in Chap. 1 to avoid treating LGB and/or T+ people as a homogenous group, and also to identify whether any trends found in the mainstream IPVA literature are replicated in our findings. Whilst a range of demographic variables would be of interest, we restrict this analysis to gender, sexuality and age. These are of interest because of our previous discussions of the relevance of debates about gender to LGB and/or T+ people's experiences of IPVA; the higher rates of IPVA victimisation amongst bisexual people in previous research; and the salience of age in light of the current lack of LGBT-inclusive relationships and sex education (RSE) for children and young people in the UK.

First, analysis of gender differences enables comparison of those identifying as men (38.1% of the sample), women (48.6%) and those who we have categorised, based on their responses, as trans+ (13.4%). This latter category includes both those whose gender identities do not map straightforwardly onto a gender binary whereby one identifies as either male or female and people whose biological sex and gender identity do not align, namely, participants who have ever identified as transgender and/or those who identified as non-binary or genderqueer. Notably, in the survey we invited trans people to identify as women, men or another gender identity, and we asked a separate question about transgender identity/history. Our choice to use the recoded variable in our subsequent gender analyses, and thus to remove trans people from the 'woman' and 'man' categories, is not intended to invalidate trans people's self-identification as women or men. Rather, our intention is to avoid perpetuating the cisgender assumption and invisibilising the experiences of participants who do not fit into a cisnormative, binaried conceptualisation of gender. Tables 3.3 and 3.4 present the headline prevalence figures for the different gender groups.

Table 3.3 shows that rates of victimisation in the last 12 months of their current/most recent relationship were higher for respondents categorised as trans+ for all types of abuse; this was most marked for emotional abuse, with 64.2% of trans+ participants reporting having experienced at least one form of emotional abuse compared to 54.6% of women and 52.9% of men. Men were considerably more likely to report having experienced at least one form of sexual abuse in the last 12 months of their current/most recent relationship (39.4%, compared to 31.0% of women), while women were slightly more likely to report having experienced at least one form of physical abuse (21.4%, compared to 19.6% of men). Conversely,

Table 3.3 Prevalence of victimisation by gender identity

Form of abuse	Percentage of respondents who have experienced any behaviour in the last 12 months of their current/most recent relationship (valid n)				Percentage of respondents who have experienced any behaviour in any other same-sex/bi/trans relationship (valid n)			
	Whole sample	Man	Woman	Trans+	Whole sample	Man	Woman	Trans+
Emotional	54.9 (537)	52.9 (206)	54.6 (262)	64.2 (67)	65.0 (323)	64.5 (138)	65.8 (149)	64.7 (34)
Financial	27.8 (724)	27.8 (273)	26.3 (361)	33.3 (87)	35.1 (542)	35.0 (214)	35.2 (264)	32.8 (61)
Physical	21.0 (675)	19.6 (245)	21.4 (341)	24.4 (86)	39.7 (486)	40.7 (204)	38.9 (226)	37.0 (54)
Sexual	35.2 (687)	39.4 (249)	31.0 (345)	40.7 (91)	48.7 (439)	47.9 (194)	49.5 (194)	51.0 (49)
Combined	64.3 (441)	63.1 (157)	62.3 (215)	74.1 (58)	70.0 (223)	68.6 (102)	71.9 (96)	66.7 (24)

Table 3.4 Prevalence of perpetration by gender identity

Form of abuse	Percentage of respondents who have used any behaviour in the last 12 months of their current/most recent relationship (valid n)				Percentage of respondents who have used any behaviour in any other same-sex/bi/trans relationship (valid n)			
	Whole sample	Man	Woman	Trans+	Whole sample	Man	Woman	Trans+
Emotional	44.9 (583)	45.2 (221)	44.6 (287)	45.2 (73)	44.3 (409)	46.4 (168)	46.9 (192)	25.5 (47)
Financial	20.1 (726)	23.0 (270)	18.7 (363)	16.7 (90)	19.3 (596)	25.0 (224)	17.7 (294)	9.2 (76)
Physical	16.0 (667)	19.8 (253)	12.8 (329)	18.1 (83)	26.7 (544)	31.9 (213)	24.3 (267)	16.1 (62)
Sexual	16.1 (684)	19.8 (252)	13.5 (342)	14.9 (87)	20.0 (544)	28.0 (207)	15.7 (268)	13.4 (67)
Combined	55.4 (484)	57.3 (185)	52.3 (239)	60.3 (58)	48.2 (326)	50.7 (140)	51.4 (148)	24.3 (37)

when examining any previous same-sex, bisexual and/or trans relationship, the percentages are very similar across gender identities.

With regard to perpetration, some starker gender differences appear, though not entirely consistently (see Table 3.4).

For physical, sexual and financial abuse, men were consistently most likely to report having enacted at least one behaviour; this was most marked for previous same-sex, bisexual and/or trans relationships. For example, in this latter category, 28.0% of men reported having enacted at least one or more sexual behaviour, compared to 15.7% of women and 13.4% of trans+ respondents. Yet, for emotional abuse, the percentage was very similar across all three gender groups for current/most recent relationships. The picture for trans+ respondents was more mixed: whereas their overall rate of perpetration in the last 12 months of their current/most recent relationship was the highest of all three gender groups (based on the combined abuse scale; 60.3%), when looking at previous same-sex, bisexual and/or trans relationships their rates were consistently the lowest, and often markedly so.

Thus, contrary to IPVA scholars who too hastily suggest that gender has no explanatory power when studying IPVA in LGB and/or T+ people's relationships, we argue that there are some pertinent gendered findings to note. Most notable are the generally higher rates of perpetration amongst men and higher rates of victimisation amongst trans+ respondents. Importantly though, the findings do not reveal wholly consistent gendered patterns across current/most recent and any previous same-sex, bisexual and/or trans relationships.

Secondly, comparison of headline prevalence by sexuality found that those identifying as bisexual were more likely (71.2%, compared to 64.3% of the sample overall) to report having experienced at least one type of violence or 'abusive' behaviour in the last 12 months of their current/most recent relationship. Further, bisexuals have the highest rates of victimisation in each of the four categories of IPVA (see Table 3.5). This supports the findings of research in the UK (ONS 2018) and in the USA (Messinger 2011; Walters et al. 2013) which similarly finds the highest rates of victimisation amongst bisexual people, and particularly bisexual women. For brevity, we do not report here on previous same-sex, bisexual and/or transgender relationships.

Turning to perpetration, respondents identifying as queer were most likely to report having used at least one of each of the categories of behav-

Table 3.5 Prevalence of victimisation by sexuality in the last 12 months of respondents' current/most recent relationship

| Form of abuse | Percentage of respondents who have experienced any behaviour in the *last 12 months of their current/most recent relationship* (valid *n*) | | | | | |
	Whole sample	Lesbian/gay woman	Gay man	Bisexual	Queer	Other[a]
Emotional	54.9 (537)	52.5 (221)	53.6 (181)	65.1 (63)	58.1 (31)	45.8 (24)
Financial	27.8 (724)	26.0 (296)	26.2 (237)	34.4 (96)	32.6 (43)	28.1 (32)
Physical	21.0 (675)	20.4 (285)	17.7 (215)	31.0 (87)	21.1 (33)	21.2 (33)
Sexual	35.2 (687)	30.9 (288)	39.5 (220)	43.3 (90)	30.8 (39)	30.0 (30)
Combined	64.3 (441)	61.0 (182)	64.7 (136)	71.2 (52)	62.5 (24)	63.6 (22)

[a]'Other' includes respondents who identified with multiple sexual identities; those who rejected any labels or described a more fluid sexuality; and those who were unsure/questioning their sexuality. Additional sexual identities that were named included pansexual and asexual. We included 'homosexual' as a category, but because only ten respondents selected this option, we have excluded it from this table. Thirty-two respondents identified as heterosexual, but only small numbers answered questions about their experience and/or use of violence and 'abusive' behaviours; therefore they too have been omitted

Table 3.6 Prevalence of perpetration by sexuality in the last 12 months of respondents' current/most recent relationship

| Form of abuse | Percentage of respondents who have used any behaviour in the *last 12 months of their current/most recent relationship* (valid *n*) | | | | | |
	Whole sample	Lesbian/gay woman	Gay man	Bisexual	Queer	Other
Emotional	44.9 (583)	41.7 (240)	45.4 (194)	49.4 (79)	51.6 (31)	45.8 (24)
Financial	20.1 (726)	18.2 (297)	20.7 (237)	19.4 (93)	34.1 (44)	15.6 (32)
Physical	16.0 (667)	11.2 (276)	18.5 (222)	19.5 (87)	27.3 (33)	20.7 (29)
Sexual	16.1 (684)	13.0 (284)	18.6 (221)	17.8 (90)	19.0 (42)	22.2 (27)
Combined	55.4 (484)	51.5 (206)	56.2 (162)	60.0 (65)	71.4 (21)	58.8 (17)

iour in the last 12 months of their current/most recent relationship, except sexual abuse, which was highest among those identifying as other. The sub-sample size for both queer and other respondents is very small, however. Rates of perpetration were lowest in all categories for lesbians/gay women, while for gay men the prevalence figures were slightly higher than in the overall sample (see Table 3.6).

Finally, when making comparisons across age groups, only data pertaining to the last 12 months of respondents' current or most recent rela-

Table 3.7 Prevalence of victimisation by age in the last 12 months of respondents' current/most recent relationship

Form of abuse	Percentage of respondents who have experienced any behaviour in the *last 12 months of their current/most recent relationship* (valid *n*)					
	Whole sample	16–24 years	25–34 years	35–44 years	45–54 years	55 years and over[a]
Emotional	54.9 (537)	58.7 (121)	53.6 (168)	51.1 (123)	59.3 (81)	53.5 (43)
Financial	27.8 (724)	20.6 (165)	27.4 (212)	35.5 (169)	28.2 (110)	26.9 (67)
Physical	21.0 (675)	23.2 (155)	20.6 (194)	21.5 (158)	22.1 (101)	14.3 (63)
Sexual	35.2 (687)	37.6 (157)	35.7 (210)	38.5 (156)	26.4 (106)	35.1 (57)
Combined	64.3 (441)	68.0 (103)	63.0 (138)	61.5 (96)	63.5 (63)	70.0 (30)

[a]Due to there being small numbers of respondents aged 65 years and over, this age group has been combined with the 55–64 years age group

tionship is used. Lifetime prevalence figures have been excluded from this analysis because these are likely to be skewed by the number of relationships and duration of relationships that older respondents will have had; hence, a focus on a specific time frame provides a more valid age comparison.

For victimisation prevalence, Table 3.7 does not show any clearly defined patterns between age and experiencing one or more 'abusive' behaviours. In terms of the overall, combined scale which encompasses all categories of behaviours, those in the oldest (aged 55 years and over; 70.0%) followed by the youngest (16–24 years; 68.0%) age groups were most likely to report experiencing one or more behaviours. Findings from the Crime Survey for England and Wales (CSEW) show that 20–24-year-olds are most likely to report experiencing domestic abuse (ONS 2018), and this is therefore, to some extent, reflected in the elevated rates of prevalence for 16–24-year-olds in our sample. This is reinforced by physical abuse being most commonly reported amongst this age group (23.2%). Financial abuse is least reported by 16–24-year-olds (20.6%), but this might reflect young people's relationships typically having fewer shared finances.

With regard to perpetration, Table 3.8 indicates a linear relationship between the proportion of different age groups that reported having used one or more of any of the emotional, financial, physical and/or sexual behaviours on the combined scale, with this figure consistently reducing

Table 3.8 Prevalence of perpetration by age in the last 12 months of respondents' current/most recent relationship

Form of abuse	Percentage of respondents who have used any behaviour in the *last 12 months of their current/most recent relationship* (valid *n*)					
	Whole sample	16–24 years	25–34 years	35–44 years	45–54 years	55 years and over
Emotional	44.9 (583)	44.2 (138)	48.8 (172)	44.3 (140)	46.6 (88)	31.8 (44)
Financial	20.1 (726)	16.5 (158)	20.9 (215)	25.1 (175)	16.5 (109)	19.1 (68)
Physical	16.0 (667)	20.1 (149)	14.2 (197)	16.1 (155)	16.5 (103)	11.3 (62)
Sexual	16.1 (684)	20.6 (160)	15.2 (204)	12.4 (161)	15.7 (102)	17.9 (56)
Combined	55.4 (484)	57.5 (120)	57.0 (142)	55.6 (117)	55.2 (67)	43.2 (37)

as age increased. The patterns for specific types of abuse did not follow this same linear pattern, but notably those aged 16–24 years were more likely to have reported using physical (20.1%) or sexual (20.6%) behaviours compared to all other age groups.

In summary—and remembering that ours is a sample drawn from the general population and not a clinical sample—the rates of what we could, at face value, term 'victimisation' and 'perpetration' are very high. However, we are very deliberately *not* claiming that the majority of our sample consists of victims and/or perpetrators of domestic violence and abuse, since these headline prevalence figures tell us very little about the nature, dynamics and impacts of individual behaviours, and what they mean in the context of people's relationships. They do, however, suggest some patterns that are in need of closer examination. The first relates to trans+ people's more prevalent experiences of victimisation. The second relates to cisgender men's generally higher rates of perpetration, consistent with a feminist gendered analysis of DVA. The third relates to our findings lending further support for previous research that has found that bisexual people report disproportionately higher rates of victimisation, but also our more uncharted finding that the prevalence of perpetration was highest amongst queer respondents, which needs further examination. The final point relates to the greater likelihood of victimisation experiences among the youngest and oldest age groups, and also the higher rates of enacting physically and sexually 'abusive' behaviours among 16–24-year-olds. These findings reinforce the importance of not treating LGB and/or T+ people as a homogenous group, and particularly of producing knowledge that visibilises those whose gender identities fall outside of the cisgender male/female gender binary.

To continue the task of queering and problematising our headline prevalence figures, we next analyse the intensity (by which we mean the number of different IPVA behaviours that are reported, and how frequently they were experienced and/or enacted) and the nature of the perpetration reported and the characteristics of those who reported using the most violence and 'abusive' behaviours. Owing to space constraints, we focus mainly on data about perpetration, although some contextualising discussion of the victimisation data is offered.

3.3 Queering 'Headline' Prevalence Figures (2): The Nature of LGB and/or T People's Use of Violence and 'Abusive' Behaviours

We begin this section with a synopsis of the data about victimisation in order to give a fuller picture of the sample, but also because, as we shall later discuss, respondents commonly reported both having experienced and enacted violence and 'abusive' behaviours. As noted previously, 64.3% of the sub-sample who provided a complete set of responses about behaviours reported having experienced one or more physical, emotional, sexual and/or financial behaviours in the last 12 months of their current/most recent relationship. Participants reported having experienced up to 56 different behaviours in the last 12 months, with a mean of 4.27 behaviours (SD = 7.08). Trans+ respondents had the highest mean number of behaviours (mean = 4.88, SD = 7.76) followed by women (mean = 4.59, SD = 7.92) and, lastly, men (mean = 3.59, SD = 5.41). Frequency scores for victimisation and perpetration were also computed, factoring in not only how many behaviours were reported, but how frequently they were each used: the gender patterns mirrored those found when only the number of behaviours was accounted for.

Regarding sexuality, the mean number of behaviours experienced in respondents' current/most recent relationships was highest for bisexual respondents (mean = 5.02, SD = 7.21), followed next by lesbians/gay women (mean = 4.92, SD = 8.72), but this order was reversed when frequency scores were considered, indicating that lesbians/gay women were subjected to violence and 'abusive' behaviours more frequently than bisexual respondents were. Age patterns were less clear-cut, but mirroring the headline prevalence figures, the highest mean number of behaviours experienced was reported by those aged 55 years and over (mean = 4.80, SD = 7.32), followed by 16–24-year-olds (mean = 4.59, SD = 7.69). However, when the frequency score is considered, 16–24-year-olds reported being subjected to 'abusive' behaviours more frequently than any other age group. Emotional behaviours were most frequently reported, with withholding affection being most commonly reported (35.3%). However, the most common ten behaviours experienced include one each of physical, sexual and financial behaviours too, with 25.6% reporting that they had been regularly insulted or put down and 15.7% reporting having been slapped, pushed or shoved.

In contrast to victimisation, perpetration was reported at lower rates of intensity. The maximum number of behaviours that participants reported using in the last 12 months of their current/most recent relationship was 17, with a mean of 1.94 behaviours (SD = 2.95). Trans+ participants used, on average, the highest number of behaviours (mean = 2.55, SD = 3.37), followed by men (mean = 1.98, SD = 2.83) and women (mean = 1.77, SD = 2.92). Again, the frequency scores reflected the same pattern. An independent-samples t test was conducted to compare means for cisgender men and women. No statistically significant differences between men and women were found in relation to victimisation or perpetration intensity ($t(340.112) = -1.804$, $p > 0.05$). This seems surprising, given that the mean frequency score for women's victimisation is considerably higher (mean = 8.39, SD = 21.05) than for men (mean = 5.34, SD = 11.08); however, the large standard deviations suggest that, especially for women, the mean is being skewed by a small number of respondents who reported very high levels of victimisation. It was not possible to include the trans+ sub-sample in the t test analysis because of its much smaller size ($n = 58$). However, more research with trans+ people is needed, with larger samples that would engender greater confidence in the findings yielded.

For sexuality, the mean number of behaviours used in the last 12 months of respondents' current/most recent relationships was highest for queer (mean = 3.64, SD = 4.65) respondents followed by bisexual (mean = 2.29, SD = 2.95) respondents. Clearly, bisexual respondents' experience and enactment of violence and 'abusive' behaviours require further research, given that there is mounting evidence of bisexual people's relationships being more likely to involve IPVA. Age patterns for perpetration showed very little variability, and the linear relationship between age and headline prevalence (for the combined abuse scale) highlighted in Sect. 3.2 was not replicated in this more nuanced intensity data.

The distinctions between the victimisation and perpetration prevalence figures problematise any notion that they describe the same phenomenon, since victimisation intensity is typically higher than perpetration intensity. Table 3.9 provides a more comprehensive breakdown, showing that where perpetration had been disclosed, it was most common for only one behaviour to have been reported. Only 3.3% of the sample reported having used ten or more different behaviours, compared to 12.8% of the sample who reported having experienced ten or more different behaviours.

In terms of which behaviours were most commonly reported, a mix of emotional and financial behaviours predominated. The most prevalent

Table 3.9 Number of different behaviours used in the last 12 months of respondents' current/most recent relationship

Total number of emotional, financial, physical and/or sexual behaviours used	Number of participants (valid n = 484)	Valid %	Cumulative %
0	216	44.6	44.6
1	87	18.0	62.6
2	57	11.8	74.4
3	32	6.6	81.0
4	23	4.8	85.7
5	13	2.7	88.4
6–9	40	8.3	96.7
10–17	16	3.3	100.0

was withholding affection, which 26.7% of participants reported having enacted at least once in the last 12 months of their current or most recent relationship (see Table 3.10). There are commonalities here with Donovan and Hester's COHSAR research, which found that 13.8% of respondents had insulted/put their partner down and 10.1% had frightened them with things they said/did in the last 12 months (2014, p. 117).

However, part of queering quantitative tools, including our own, involves recognising that survey items, devoid of context, can be interpreted in numerous ways. For example, it would be problematic to sug-

Table 3.10 Most common behaviours used in the last 12 months of respondents' current/most recent relationship

Behaviour	Valid n	% used at least once in the last 12 months	% once or twice	% monthly	% weekly	% daily
Withheld your affection from your partner (E)	752	26.7	21.7	3.4	1.4	0.1
Accused them of being unfaithful (E)	761	12.6	11.1	1.0	0.5	0.0
Regularly insulted or put them down (E)	763	12.2	10.1	1.6	0.6	0.0
Slapped/pushed/shoved them (P)	749	12.1	11.6	0.5	0.0	0.0
Frightened them with things you said/did (E)	751	10.2	9.2	1.0	0.0	0.0
Gave your partner pocket money (F)	745	8.3	4.9	2.4	0.8	0.3
Had sex with your partner when they were drunk/asleep (S)	745	7.2	5.9	1.1	0.1	0.0
Required them to account for all their expenditure (F)	746	7.1	6.1	1.0	0.0	0.0
Regularly expected your partner to pay for most of the joint or relationship expenses (F)	746	5.9	3.3	1.3	0.8	0.6
Used their education/intelligence against them (E)	759	5.6	5.1	0.5	0.0	0.0

E = emotional; P = physical; S = sexual; F = financial

gest that withholding affection is always used in an abusive way, such as to punish or manipulate a partner. Rather, it may also be used by a partner who is being victimised and who no longer trusts or feels affectionate towards their abuser; or it could reflect one or both partners withdrawing from intimacy if a relationship encounters difficulty or is in the process of ending, as would have been likely when considering the last 12 months of a relationship that, for those reporting on their most recent rather than current relationship, was coming to an end. Similarly, free-text comments and interview data indicate that respondents who reported that they had 'frightened [their partner] with things [they] said/did' included within this self-harm and episodes of poor mental health which they recognised would have been frightening for their partner to witness, but where there had been no intention to frighten their partner. In hindsight, we could have added 'deliberately' to the wording of this item to make intent a prerequisite. However, items which were arguably more unequivocal, such as 'regularly insulted them or put them down' and 'slapped/pushed/ shoved them', also appeared in the ten most commonly reported behaviours (see Table 3.10).

We asked about a range of identity abuse behaviours, including using their partner's (or having a partner use their) age, disability, sexuality, gender identity and social class against them, but the only one which appears in the most common perpetration behaviours is identity abuse related to education/intelligence. This mirrors the most common form of identity abuse reported in the COHSAR study (Donovan and Hester 2014). In the follow-up interviews, participants described being belittled or ridiculed for being too intelligent or qualified, or conversely for not being intelligent or educated enough. These findings are a reminder of the importance of an intersectional analysis which does not restrict its focus to identity abuse related to sexuality and/or gender identity. To queer knowledge about IPVA is thus to include aspects that are specific to sexuality and/or gender identity, but without assuming that these aspects of identities are always the ones which are most implicated in LGB and/or T+ people's experiences of IPVA.

With regard to how frequently these behaviours were reportedly used, as noted previously, it was rare for violence and 'abusive' behaviours to be reported as having been used more than once or twice in the 12-month time frame that we asked about. Some of the financial behaviours in Table 3.10 were reported by a very small proportion of participants as having been used on a weekly or even daily basis (e.g. 'regularly expected your partner to pay for most of the joint or relationship expenses' was reportedly used at least weekly by 1.4% of participants). However, this might reflect how finances were organised in participants' intimate relationships and the impacts of those practices for people's day-to-day lives. The other more frequently reported item—albeit by very small proportions of the sample—was withholding affection, reported to have been enacted at least weekly by 1.5% of participants.

In summary, closer analysis of our prevalence figures presents a significant challenge to IPVA scholars whose analyses reify such 'headline' figures without fully unpacking them. Our analysis indicates that headline victimisation and headline perpetration figures are not comparable: respondents report enacting fewer perpetration behaviours and at lower rates of frequency than is the case for victimisation experiences. Thus, there is less variability in the cohort of respondents that is enacting IPVA behaviours, and this has implications for what is and is not possible statistically within the ensuing analysis. Mirroring the headline prevalence figures, trans+ people experienced IPVA behaviours at higher rates of intensity, but they also appeared to enact them more frequently too, followed next by male respondents. Bisexual people also seem to experience IPVA behaviours at higher rates of intensity, while queer and bisexual people appear to enact violence and 'abusive' behaviours with higher intensity. Age patterns were less distinct, particularly for perpetration. Importantly, the most commonly reported behaviours across the sample, whilst dominated by emotional behaviours, included physical, sexual and financial behaviours too.

However, as we have highlighted, achieving precise and unambiguous measurement is very difficult—arguably even impossible—in IPVA research, largely because a single item can include a spectrum of severity and different meanings and motivations. This is not only a limitation of our survey instrument (although there are items that in hindsight could be improved), but rather reflects the limitations of quantitative tools for measuring highly qualitative experiences. Therefore, one of our key messages is that we have to be very cautious about what we take from quantitative data in isolation, as we saw in Chap. 2 when we examined what Jack meant by 'threats to kill', and as we shall see in the case studies in Chap. 4.

3.4   Queering Typologies of IPVA

It has already been established in our data that 'victims' and 'perpetrators' are far from homogenous, and that relying on headline prevalence figures alone reproduces the limitations of Conflict Tactics Scale–based approaches by conflating one-off incidents of violence and 'abusive' behaviour with chronic, high-intensity abuse which has highly pervasive impacts (see Chap. 2). Next, we offer an exploratory analysis of whether different types of IPVA identified by Johnson (2008) can be found in our sample. In particular, we examine whether we can differentiate between situational couple violence (SCV), coercively controlling violence (CCV) and violent resistance (VR) within our sample, which, as we shall see in Chap. 5, has implications for providing LGB and/or T+ people with appropriate responses to different types of IPVA.

We first explain how we identified subgroups for high/low/no perpetration and victimisation, noting overlaps between these groups which underline the limitations of a rigid victim/perpetrator binary. We then explore three themes within our survey data which are relevant to the theoretical underpinnings of Johnson's (2008) typology; namely, reported motives for using violence and 'abusive' behaviours; reported impacts of victimisation; and indicators of the dynamics of power and control in respondents' relationships. Throughout, we identify the challenges of trying to categorise respondents based on quantitative data alone, even when using our more complex and detailed survey instrument.

3.4.1   Moving Beyond Treating 'Perpetrators' as a Homogenous Group: Identifying Subgroups

To move beyond seeing perpetrators as a homogenous group, we divided the sample into three subgroups: high perpetration, low perpetration and no perpetration. Moreover, whilst discussed in less detail in this book, high victimisation, low victimisation and no victimisation subgroups have also been created. Focussing on the extremes of the sample enables closer examination of the characteristics of these groups, but importantly too, how they differ from the majority of participants who reported using (or experiencing) fewer behaviours.

The variable used to categorise respondents into the subgroups was the total number of emotional, physical, sexual and/or financial 'abusive' behaviours that they reported having experienced or enacted, respectively, in the last 12 months of their current/most recent relationship. We did consider using the frequency score variable which takes into account both the number of IPVA behaviours and how frequently they were reportedly experienced or enacted, but comparison between the two variables found that there were no notable differences between them. Thus, for ease of use, we have continued to use the total number of IPVA behaviours.

To create the high victimisation subgroup, a cut-off point of 10 or more behaviours was applied. This captured 12.8% of those who provided a complete set of responses about their experience of emotional, physical, sexual and/or financial behaviours in the last 12 months of their current or most recent relationship (n = 431), a subgroup of 55 participants. The low victimisation subgroup (one to nine behaviours) is much larger, comprising 222 participants (see Table 3.11). This cut-off of 10 is informed by analysis conducted in the COHSAR study (Donovan and Hester 2014), where approximately 10% of the sample was classified as reporting both high victimisation and high impacts of victimisation, which Donovan and Hester (2014) argued was indicative of CCV victimisation.

For the high perpetration subgroup, a cut off of six or more violent or 'abusive' behaviours was applied, capturing 11.6% of the sample (n = 486); a subgroup of 56 participants. Again, the low perpetration subgroup (one to five behaviours) is much larger, comprising 212 participants (see Table 3.11). This lower cut-off of six or more behaviours was chosen because rates of reported perpetration were lower than rates of reported victimisation. Similar numbers of participants and proportions of the sample fall into the high perpetration and high victimisation subgroups, respectively, accounting for just over a one in ten of all respondents who provided sufficient data,

Table 3.11 Summary of original victimisation and perpetration subgroups

	Victimisation		
	High (10+ behaviours reported in the last 12 months of current/most recent relationship)	Low (1–9 behaviours reported in the last 12 months of current/most recent relationship)	None
Number of respondents	55	222	154
% of those who reported any victimisation[a]	19.9	80.1	NA
% of valid sample (n = 431)	12.8	51.5	35.7
	Perpetration		
	High (6+ behaviours reported in the last 12 months of current/most recent relationship)	Low (1–5 behaviours reported in the last 12 months of current/most recent relationship)	None
Number of respondents	56	212	218
% of those who reported any perpetration[a]	20.9	79.1	NA
% of valid sample (n = 486)	11.6	43.6	44.9

[a]Based on reporting 1+ emotional, physical, sexual and/or financial behaviours in the last 12 months of respondents' current or most recent relationship

and approximately a fifth of those who reported experiencing or enacting one or more behaviours, respectively.

During the analysis, we identified 16 respondents who fell into both the high perpetration and high victimisation subgroups. This is not surprising because, overall, 69.7% of those who reported enacting at least one IPVA behaviour in the past 12 months also reported having experienced at least one behaviour, while 88.0% of those who reported experiencing at least one IPVA behaviour also reported having enacted at least one behaviour. In much of the IPVA literature, these cases would be classified as 'mutual abuse'. Yet, as we have noted previously, the term 'mutual abuse' tells us nothing about—and indeed risks misrepresenting—the power dynamics of the relationship (Hodes and Mennicke 2019), as we demonstrate via our case studies in Chap. 4. A decision was made to

Table 3.12 Final high victimisation and high perpetration subgroups

	High victimisation	High perpetration
Original high subgroup size	55	56
Final subgroup size after overlapping cases removed	39	40
% of valid sample	9.0	8.3

remove this small group of overlapping participants (the high victimisation–high perpetration subgroup) to enable the high perpetration and high victimisation subgroups to be independent of one another. The final high victimisation and high perpetration subgroups are presented in Table 3.12.

A limitation of this analysis is that the sizes of the various subgroups are much smaller than the overall sample. This has restricted the statistical analyses that can be reliably performed, meaning that significance testing has not been possible in most of this subsequent analysis. However, our aim is not to make definitive claims with our data, but rather to explore different and more nuanced ways of analysing our data that trouble more simplistic uses of headline prevalence figures. It is our hope that other IPVA researchers will be encouraged to replicate these or similar analyses—and with larger samples which enable statistical power to be retained when subgroups are compared.

Some of the key demographic trends within our subgroups are:

• Reflecting our previously discussed findings, a higher proportion of men (9.7%) than women (7.5%) are in the high perpetration subgroup. Inversely, women are more likely to be in the high victimisation subgroup (10.2% of women compared to 7.6% of men).
• Trans+ respondents are slightly over-represented in the high perpetration group, comprising 14.3% of this subgroup, compared to 13.4% of the overall sample.
• Respondents who identified their sexuality as bisexual or queer are over-represented in the high perpetration group compared to the overall sample; this is most marked for queer people (12.5% compared to 4.4% in the sample), although numbers are small ($n = 21$). Bisexual people are over-represented in the high victimisation subgroup

(18.2% compared to 11.9% in the overall sample), as are lesbians (34.5% compared to 26.9% in the overall sample).

- Respondents in the high perpetration subgroup are more likely to be aged 40 years and over (40.0%), compared to 33.5% in the population as a whole.
- Those in the high perpetration subgroup are less likely to have an undergraduate or postgraduate degree (52.5%), compared to those in the low perpetration (60.2%) and no perpetration (58.7%) subgroups. However, all of these figures are higher than that for the high victimisation subgroup (44.5%).
- The high perpetration group are least likely to be reporting about their first same-sex, bisexual and/or trans relationship (5.0%, compared to 11.8% in the overall sample), whereas this figure is highest in the high victimisation subgroup (20.5%). This points to less experienced LGB and/or T+ partners' potential vulnerability to being subjected to the 'experiential power' (Donovan et al. 2014) of more experienced LGB and/or T+ partners, as discussed in Chap. 4.

3.4.2   Looking for Johnson's Typology in the Coral Project Data

The subdivision of the sample into the subgroups introduced earlier underlines the arguments of other scholars (Hodes and Mennicke 2019; Stark 2007) that most IPVA that is observed in general population samples is of low intensity and severity. In this section, we analyse three aspects of our data—motives for perpetration; impacts of victimisation; and power and control dynamics—to probe further into the nature and dynamics of IPVA, power and control across the subgroups. This enables resonances with, and divergences from, Johnson's (2008) typology of IPVA to be identified.

3.4.2.1   Motives for Using 'Abusive' Behaviours

Respondents who reported having ever used one or more violent or 'abusive' behaviours were asked to choose all that applied from a list of possible reasons for their behaviour. Respondents were not asked to give motives for each 'abusive' behaviour used as this would have been too onerous in an already long questionnaire. Consequently, our approach yields insights into the wider relationship context, although where respondents have selected multiple motives, the relative weighting of each is not captured. This, however, would be difficult to do using quantitative methods alone, given that reported motives can shift over time as individuals' perceptions of their relationship, their partner and themselves change.

Only 106 respondents answered these questions. We can only speculate, but this may be because this question was towards the end of a long questionnaire, or perhaps because they did not want to acknowledge their reasons for using 'abusive' behaviours. Motives for the high and low perpetration subgroups are presented in Table 3.13. It would have also been insightful to compare these responses to those in the high victimisation subgroup, in order to explore whether the motives selected for any IPVA behaviours used correspond to VR, such as protecting themselves or their property/pets. Unfortunately, this was not possible because hardly any respondents in the high victimisation subgroup provided motives data.

For the low perpetration subgroup, the most common motives for using 'abusive' behaviours were 'Because you were unhappy in the relationship' (11.8%), 'You didn't feel good enough/felt insecure' (11.8%) and 'Because of your emotional problems' (9.0%). Controlling motives such as jealousy or a desire to punish and self-defensive or self-protective motives were seldom reported. This, combined with the lower-level use of violence and 'abusive' behaviours, indicates that what dominates in the low perpetration subgroup is SCV.

Contrastingly, the high perpetration subgroup includes motives associated with both CCV and VR. Motives that are associated with being controlling are much more common amongst the high perpetration subgroup; for example, 20.0% of the high perpetration subgroup reported the motive, 'Made you feel in control' and 12.5% 'Because you felt undermined or your authority had been challenged' compared to only 0.9% of the low perpetration subgroup in both cases. However, self-defensive motives were almost five times higher in the high perpetration subgroup (20.0% reported 'To protect yourself from harm', compared to

Table 3.13 Motives for using violence and 'abusive' behaviours—comparing high perpetration and low perpetration subgroups

Motives	High perpetration (%) (*n* = 40)	Low perpetration (%) (*n* = 212)
Because you were unhappy in the relationship	27.5	11.8
Because of your emotional problems	27.5	9.0
To retaliate against them	22.5	4.7
You didn't feel good enough/felt insecure	20.0	11.8
To protect yourself from them	20.0	4.2
Made you feel in control	20.0	0.9
Because you were unhappy in work/life	17.5	5.2
Because you didn't know what else to do	17.5	5.2
Because you didn't trust them	17.5	4.2
Because you were jealous/possessive	17.5	2.4
Because they betrayed/rejected you	12.5	3.3
Because you felt undermined or your authority had been challenged	12.5	0.9
Because you loved/cared for them	10.0	5.2
Because of your alcohol/drugs use	10.0	2.8
Because they were laughing at you	10.0	2.4
Because of your previous experience of abuse	10.0	2.4
Because they hit you first	10.0	1.9
To punish them	10.0	1.9
Because that's how it is in your relationship	10.0	0.5
Because that's how you were brought up	10.0	0.9
Sometimes you get angry and can't control what you do	7.5	2.4
To stop them leaving you	7.5	0.5
To protect your property/pets	5.0	0.0
To prevent them harming themselves	2.5	1.4
To protect your children/family/friends	0.0	1.4
Because of trans/bi/homophobia you've experienced	0.0	0.0

4.2% in the low perpetration subgroup). This indicates heterogeneity amongst the high perpetration subgroup: some respondents are motivated by control and entitlement, typical of CCV perpetration, while others appear to be enacting violence and 'abusive' behaviours in a self-protective way, potentially consistent with VR and indicating the creation of space for reaction, which we discuss in Chap. 4.

Further, the high perpetration subgroup appears to be a group with more complex needs: using 'abusive' behaviours due to their emotional problems (27.5%), their alcohol or drug use (10.0%), their unhappiness with their work or life (17.5%), their previous experiences of abuse (10.0%) and their upbringing (10.0%) were all most frequently reported amongst the high perpetration subgroup. No respondents selected 'Because of homo/bi/transphobia you've experienced'; this challenges the minority stress thesis discussed in Chap. 1, although we should not assume that individuals have full insight into the reasons for their behaviour. The different motives behind the use of 'abusive' behaviours have implications for the interventions which are likely to meet the needs of different types of perpetrators, as we return to in Chap. 5.

3.4.2.2 Impacts of Victimisation

Secondly, impacts of victimisation are considered, using a wide range of items. This is modelled on the COHSAR survey (Donovan and Hester 2014) and recognises the need to look beyond only physical harm (see Donovan and Barnes 2019). Including the perpetration subgroups in this analysis is an unusual step, yet this is key to troubling the victim/perpetrator binary by recognising that one should not consider perpetration behaviours in isolation (see Dobash and Dobash 2004).

One possible measure of the extent of victimisation impact is how many different adverse impacts respondents reported. Mean numbers of impacts were compared across the high victimisation (mean = 9.69, SD = 6.37), low victimisation (mean = 2.12, SD = 4.04) and high perpetration (mean = 6.30, SD = 6.07) subgroups. This shows that, as expected, the high victimisation group typically reports the most extensive impacts, and yet the figure for the high perpetration subgroup is almost three times as much as for the low victimisation subgroup. As with the motives data, the impacts data for the low victimisation subgroup resonates strongly with SCV. As well as reporting relatively few impacts, other key indicators are that the erosion of self-esteem, fear and entrapment that are characteristic of coercive control (Stark 2007) are seldom reported. For example, 9.0% of the low victimisation subgroup felt trapped compared to 48.7% of the high victimisation—and 27.5% of the high perpetration—subgroups (see Table 3.14). Notably though, small proportions of the low victimisation subgroup do report adverse impacts, hence it is important not to over-rely on broad trends and subsequently overlook the needs of outliers.

Conversely, the high victimisation subgroup reports a wider range of impacts, at much higher rates. The most common impacts include feeling worthless/loss of confidence (64.1%), losing trust in their partner (64.1%) and feeling that they had to watch what they said/did (61.5%). The least common impacts were receiving physical injuries and being in fear of one's life, and one in ten of the high victimisation subgroup selected each of these. Certainly, whilst not uniformly, this supports the suggestion that the high victimisation subgroup has disproportionately experienced CCV (see Table 3.14).

Table 3.14 Impacts of victimisation—comparing high victimisation, low victimisation and high perpetration subgroups

Impact[a]	High victimisation (%) (n = 40)	Low victimisation (%) (n = 222)	High perpetration (%) (n = 39)
Felt worthless/lost confidence	64.1	9.9	45.0
Stopped trusting your partner	64.1	10.8	40.0
Felt you had to watch what you said or did	61.5	13.5	35.0
Felt angry, stupid or ashamed	59.0	12.6	37.5
Felt sadness/shock	51.3	13.1	40.0
Felt anxiety or panic or lost concentration	48.7	13.1	40.0
Felt depressed	48.7	9.9	35.0
Felt trapped	48.7	9.0	27.5
Felt scared/frightened	43.6	5.0	25.0
Felt isolated/stopped going out	46.2	5.4	17.5
Felt suicidal	33.3	2.3	17.5
Feared for your life	10.3	1.8	7.5
Received physical injuries	10.3	1.4	5.0

[a]This is not an exhaustive list, but rather those that are most salient to this analysis

However, whereas one might expect that members of the high perpetration subgroup are experiencing 'abusive' behaviours in the form of VR, this is not the case, and instead there are many similarities with the high victimisation subgroup, albeit with generally lower levels of fear and entrapment. This suggests that some of the high perpetration subgroup may be enacting VR themselves, in response to coercively controlling partners. Again, therefore, this shows that even when using subgroups which enable the survey data to be divided up in more nuanced ways, homogeneity within categories cannot be assumed.

3.4.2.3 Power and Control—Who Makes the Decisions?

We turn thirdly to how power and control operate in relationships in an attempt to overcome the limitations of much research which focuses on specific incidents of violence and 'abuse' rather than the wider relationship context. As part of our exploratory approach, we asked various questions about control, conflict and relationship expectations. We focus here on our key findings about decision-making in respondents' intimate relationships and we explore relationships between this and the experience and/or enactment of 'abusive' behaviours. The rationale for this analysis is to explore whether it is possible to distinguish between CCV profiles, which combine high use of 'abusive' behaviours with high levels of control, and SCV or VR profiles, which would be associated with greater equality or deprivation of autonomy, respectively (Hodes and Mennicke 2019; Johnson 2008). Further, as discussed in Chap. 1, Donovan and Hester's (2014) second relationship rule stipulates that the abusive partner will make all of the key decisions, and we are able to explore this within this sample. Clinical samples of HC male perpetrators typically show high endorsement of controlling attitudes and patriarchal entitlement (Anderson and Umberson 2001; Dobash et al. 2000; Hearn 1998), but no comparable data exists for LGB and/or T+ people who use 'abusive' behaviours in their intimate relationships.

Respondents were asked about 24 different types of decision (e.g. decisions affecting both partners to a relationship such as when to have sex and being out to people as a couple; and decisions affecting individual partners such as their clothes and hairstyle and their partner's clothes and hairstyle). They were asked both who would ideally make the final decision and who actually makes/made the final decision in their current/most recent relationship (themselves, their partner or jointly), thus providing a unique opportunity to explore whether ideal and actual decision-making correspond, or not. Three items related to parenting and children were removed because they were not applicable to the majority of the sample, leaving 21 decisions in the final analysis.

In terms of ideal decision-making, respondents overwhelmingly desired joint decision-making. Scores for both ideal and actual decision-making range from 0 to 42 (where zero would mean that the respondent did not make the final decision for any item, and 42 would involve the respondent making the final decision on all items). The mean was 21.0 (SD = 1.40)—exactly at the mid-point of the scale—meaning that respondents typically wanted to make final decisions jointly with their partner. This could reflect a social desirability bias, but it could also reflect findings particularly from research with LGB people about same-sex relationships which finds higher aspirations for relational equality and mutuality, even if this is not always realised in practice (Carrington 1999; Solomon et al. 2005; Weeks et al. 2001). Further, Barnes' (2013) qualitative analysis of 40 women's accounts of partner abuse from a female partner found that some participants described very democratic and egalitarian aspects to their relationships, alongside unequivocally abusive aspects. The mean for actual decision-making is 19.96 (SD = 3.62), indicating that respondents are, on average, most likely to actually make decisions together. The slightly lower mean for actual decision-making suggests that respondents want nominally more control than they feel they actually have. Women and trans+ respondents were slightly less likely to report actually experiencing as much control as they would ideally want, whereas ideal and actual decision-making were on a par for men.

Respondents were then split into groups based on whether, on average, they are more submissive in decision-making (low control = scores of 0–10), whether they are generally equally in control of decisions (equal control = scores of 11–21), and whether they tend to be dominant in decision-making (dominant control = scores of 22+). Notably, what is categorised as dominance in the sample is not indicative of highly controlling behaviour because few respondents ideally or actually made many sole final decisions. Rather, it shows an inclination to making more decisions independently, rather than jointly. The vast majority of respondents felt that they generally had equal control of making decisions (73.5%), and that this was also their ideal (85.9%). However, whilst this paints a broad picture of relational equality, it is also important to highlight that approximately a fifth of respondents desired equality in decision-making but did not actually experience it. Most commonly, the direction of this was that they found themselves being more dominant in actual decision-making (17.5%) rather than having less control (4.0%).

The next step was to examine the relationship between the locus of control in decision-making and the use of violence and 'abusive' behaviours. Counter-intuitively, no significant correlations were found between decision-making scores and either the number of IPVA behaviours used in the last 12 months of respondents' current/most recent relationships or the frequency score. Thus, data on relationship decision-making has not helped to predict perpetration, although that may be because equality in ideal and actual decision-making was most commonly reported. However, a moderate negative correlation was found (Pearson's $r = -0.687$, $p < 0.01$) between the number of 'abusive' behaviours experienced and the actual decision-making score. Thus, participants who experienced more intense victimisation made fewer decisions in their relationships. Indeed, the mean score for actual decision-making was 15.43 (SD = 6.49) for the high victimisation subgroup, while the high perpetration subgroup mean was 20.73 (SD = 3.98), which was only slightly higher than the sample mean. This points to loss of autonomy and micro-regulation of their day-to-day activities by their partners among the high victimisation subgroup, characteristic of Stark's (2007) concept of coercive control, whilst also supporting Donovan and Hester's (2014) concept of the abusive partner imposing the second relationship rule by making all of the decisions.

As noted earlier, exploration of this data is intended to capture something of the relationship context rather than focussing purely on the use of specific behaviours at specific moments in time. However, we also recognise that the nature of quantitative data means that this gives us an inevitably partial view. We do not know if it has been negotiated that one partner would take the lead on certain decisions, and indeed one respondent used the 'other' free-text box to indicate that they were in a relationship based on bondage, discipline, sadism and masochism (BDSM), and that as part of this consensual relationship dynamic, the dominant partner made all of the decisions. Moreover, individuals' life circumstances and relationship stages (e.g. living together or apart) will influence the extent to which some of the decisions which we asked about would be shared or would be solely made by the respondents or their partner, respectively. Furthermore, related to actual decision-making, this data relies on one partner's perceptions, and individuals may not reflect on whether their behaviour facilitated their partner in making decisions freely, or sometimes whether they themselves could make decisions autonomously. A glimpse into such dynamics is evident in the follow-up interview with Adam, a white, cisgender gay man in his mid-30s who we categorised in the qualitative analysis as a perpetrator of CCV in some of his previous relationships. He recalled:

> Um in other relationships where I've given them [former partners] some control [...] I've been sort of reaching around their shoulders and actually steering them where I wanted to go. So it looks like they're in control but I've still, you know [...] so like choosing films I pre-selected two or three which was appropriate and then 'You can choose the final' [...] or going out for dinner and 'Well I'll eat here or here, but you can choose which of those two places we'll go to'.

Technically, in such a situation, a partner of Adam's might well say that they made the final decision, and yet seeing this richer, qualitative context demonstrates that this happened in very contrived and manipulated way, rather than in a context where each partner's preferences were equally valued. Despite these limitations, having data on ideal decision-making as well as actual decision-making offers insights into any discrepancies in how respondents would ideally want power and control to operate within their intimate relationships, but in this analysis it has been more useful in identifying potential victims/survivors of CCV than it has been in differentiating between different types of IPVA that are being enacted.

3.5   Summary

This chapter set out to do two types of queering: to bring LGB and/or T+ people—and in particular their reports of enacting 'abusive' behaviours—into the IPVA literature, yet also to problematise some of the ways in which quantitative knowledge about IPVA is produced and leads to potentially misleading claims being made. In relation to bringing LGB and/or T+ people in, at the level of 'headline' prevalence figures we found that very high proportions of the sample had either experienced (64.3%) or enacted (55.4%) at least one of the large number of 'abusive' behaviours that we asked about, with emotionally 'abusive' behaviours being most common. Key findings include the heightened IPVA victimisation risks to trans+ and bisexual people, younger and older people, as well as indications of higher use of 'abusive' behaviours by trans+, bisexual and queer people and cisgender men.

Our exploratory analyses have found evidence of different types of IPVA from Johnson's (2008) typology. Importantly, most IPVA reported was of low intensity, and this applied especially to reported perpetration. Thus, analyses of motives for perpetration and impacts of victimisation suggest that the IPVA captured within the low perpetration and low victimisation subgroups is predominantly—albeit importantly, not exclusively—SCV. In contrast, there are clear indications of CCV within the high victimisation subgroup, based on the most extensive impacts of victimisation being observed and the lower input into decision-making; this points to a subgroup where experiences of entrapment and deprivation of autonomy are common. The high perpetration subgroup is more complex and heterogeneous and appears to combine those who are enacting CCV, illustrated by the higher reporting of controlling motives for their use of violence and 'abusive' behaviours, yet also those whose use of IPVA behaviours is likely to be VR and the creation of space for reaction in response to a partner who is perpetrating CCV. This is evident both because of the high levels of adverse impacts and mixture of controlling and self-defensive motives within this subgroup. This heterogeneity of IPVA has key implications for the responses required, as will be discussed in Chap. 5.

The caution that we have expressed about how our 'headline' figures should be interpreted, as well as the heterogeneity of particularly 'perpetrators' that we have found, reflects our second aim of queering how knowledge is produced about IPVA. Over the course of our analysis we have highlighted multiple issues which point to the limitations of using quantitative data alone to measure IPVA, even—indeed, perhaps especially—when using a more complex and nuanced survey instrument, as we did. These include the challenges of capturing the relationship context rather than purely specific incidents; the different ways in which survey items can be interpreted; and the high levels of missing data, which result from using a more detailed questionnaire, which in turn has implications for the robustness of the data and the claims that can be made. These are ongoing challenges for all IPVA researchers, and they point to the value of a mixed-methods approach through which qualitative explorations of relationship context can problematise the assumptions that might be made when using quantitative data alone. This argument comes to the fore in Chap. 4, where we focus in on the accounts of those who, based on their survey data, could be categorised as having engaged in 'mutual abuse', yet conversely demonstrate how their qualitative accounts indicate that they are being victimised by CCV but have been able to create space for reaction.

References

Anderson, K. L., & Umberson, D. (2001). Gendering violence: Masculinity and power in men's accounts of domestic violence. *Gender and Society, 15*(3), 358–380.

Badenes-Ribera, L., Bonilla-Campos, A., Frias-Navarro, D., Pons-Salvador, G., & Monterde-i-Bort, H. (2016). Intimate partner violence in self-identified lesbians: A systematic review of its prevalence and correlates. *Trauma, Violence, & Abuse, 17*(3), 284–297.

Ball, M. (2016). *Criminology and queer theory: Dangerous bedfellows?* Basingstoke: Palgrave Macmillan.

Barnes, R. (2013). 'She expected her women to be pretty, subservient, dinner on the table at six': Problematising the narrative of egalitarianism in lesbian relationships through accounts of woman-to-woman partner abuse. In T. Sanger

& Y. Taylor (Eds.), *Mapping intimacies: Relations, exchanges, affects* (pp. 130–149). Basingstoke: Palgrave Macmillan.

Carrington, C. (1999). *No place like home: Relationships and family life among lesbians and gay men.* London: University of Chicago Press.

Dobash, R. E., Dobash, R. P., Cavanagh, K., & Lewis, R. (2000). *Changing violent men.* London: Sage.

Dobash, R. P., & Dobash, R. E. (2004). Women's violence to men in intimate relationships: Working on a puzzle. *British Journal of Criminology, 44*(3), 324–349.

Donovan, C., & Barnes, R. (2019, July 26). Re-tangling the concept of coercive control: A view from the margins and a response to Walby and Towers (2018). *Criminology and Criminal Justice.* https://doi.org/10.1177/1748895819864622

Donovan, C., Barnes, R., & Nixon, C. (2014). *The Coral Project: Exploring abusive behaviours in lesbian, gay, bisexual and/or transgender relationships: Interim report.* Sunderland and Leicester: University of Sunderland and University of Leicester. Retrieved March 30, 2019, from https://www2.le.ac.uk/departments/criminology/documents/coral-project-interim-report

Donovan, C., & Hester, M. (2014). *Domestic violence and sexuality: What's love got to do with it?* Bristol: Policy Press.

Finneran, C., & Stephenson, R. (2012). Intimate partner violence among men who have sex with men: A systematic review. *Trauma, Violence, & Abuse, 14*(2), 168–185.

Frankland, A., & Brown, J. (2014). Coercive control in same-sex intimate partner violence. *Journal of Family Violence, 29*(1), 15–22.

Hearn, J. (1998). *The violences of men: How men talk about and how agencies respond to men's violence to women.* London: Sage.

Hester, M., Jones, C., Williamson, E., Fahmy, E., & Feder, G. (2017). Is it coercive controlling violence? A cross-sectional domestic violence and abuse survey of men attending general practice in England. *Psychology of Violence, 7*(3), 417–427.

Hodes, C., & Mennicke, A. (2019). Is it conflict or abuse? A practice note for furthering differential assessment and response. *Journal of Clinical Social Work, 47*(2), 176–184.

Johnson, M. P. (2008). *A typology of domestic violence: Intimate terrorism, violent resistance, and situational couple violence.* Boston: Northeastern University Press.

Messinger, A. M. (2011). Invisible victims: Same-sex IPV in the national violence against women survey. *Journal of Interpersonal Violence, 26*(11), 2228–2243.

Myhill, A., & Kelly, L. (2019, July 11). Counting with understanding? What is at stake in debates on researching domestic violence. *Criminology & Criminal Justice*. https://doi.org/10.1177/1748895819863098

Office for National Statistics (ONS). (2018). *Women most at risk of experiencing partner abuse in England and Wales: Years ending March 2015 to 2017*. London: ONS.

Solomon, S. E., Rothblum, E. D., & Balsam, K. F. (2005). Money, housework, sex and conflict: Same-sex couples in civil unions, those not in civil unions and heterosexual married siblings. *Sex Roles, 52*, 561–575.

Stark, E. (2007). *Coercive control: How men entrap women in personal life*. Oxford: Oxford University Press.

Walters, M. L., Chen, J., & Breiding, M. J. (2013). *The National Intimate Partner and Sexual Violence Survey (NISVS): 2010 findings on victimization by sexual orientation*. Atlanta: National Center for Injury Prevention and Control, Centers for Disease Control and Prevention.

Weeks, J., Heaphy, B., & Donovan, C. (2001). *Same-sex intimacies: Families of choice and other life experiments*. Abingdon: Routledge.

4

Barriers to Recognising Domestic Violence and Abuse: Power, Resistance and the Re-storying of 'Mutual Abuse'

Abstract Chapter 4 presents five case studies from the Coral Project's qualitative data to queer heteronormative, cisnormative narratives of intimate partner violence and abuse (IPVA) that reproduce binaries of male/female, victim/perpetrator in relation to the public story of domestic violence and abuse, and to demonstrate the importance of understanding relationship contexts before making an assessment of what type of IPVA is being used. We include an outline of how we have categorised participants' accounts, informed by Johnson's typology. Whilst interview participants for this chapter were selected because they appeared quantitatively to be 'perpetrators' of IPVA and to be in relationships characterised by mutual abuse, the selected case studies problematise these assumptions and argue for closer attention to the different kinds of IPVA that are enacted and the relationship contexts that they are enacted within. Through these case studies, we make two key points: first, that patriarchal heteronormativity and cisnormativity are relevant to the experiences of LGB and/or T+ people who are victimised by coercively controlling partners; and second, that victims/survivors who use space for reaction in response to coercively controlling partners find it difficult to recognise their victimisation, in turn inhibiting their opportunities for help-seeking.

© The Author(s) 2020   **97**
C. Donovan, R. Barnes, *Queering Narratives of Domestic Violence and Abuse*, Palgrave
Studies in Victims and Victimology, https://doi.org/10.1007/978-3-030-35403-9_4

Keywords Coercive control • Domestic violence and abuse •
Experiential power • Identity abuse • Intersectionality • Intimate
partner violence and abuse • Lesbian, gay, bisexual and/or transgender •
Love • Mutual abuse • Perpetrators • Power and control • Public story
of domestic violence and abuse • Qualitative • Relationship rules •
Resistance • Space for reaction • Typologies of domestic violence and
abuse • Victims/survivors

4.1   Introduction

In this chapter we present five case studies from the Coral Project's qualitative data to queer heteronormative, cisnormative narratives of intimate
partner violence and abuse (IPVA) and to demonstrate the importance of
understanding relationship contexts before making an assessment of what
type of IPVA is being used. This follows on from Chap. 3, where even
within the subgroup that we called 'high perpetration', there is heterogeneity of experience; and where across the sample as a whole, rates of
apparent 'mutual abuse' are exceptionally high, yet under-scrutinised.
Through re-examining some participants' use of IPVA as enacting what
we call space for reaction, we argue that the rigidity of the ideal victim/
perpetrator binary incorrectly interprets such behaviours as provocation,
discrediting the blamelessness of the victim/survivor. This, in turn, has
implications for recognition of victimisation and the operation of power
in a relationship from the perspective of the victim/survivor and of others
external to the relationship, and can act as a barrier to help-seeking.
Before we turn to the case studies, we provide an overview of the interviews and our categorisation of them.

4.2   Using Johnson's Typology to Categorise
Qualitative Accounts of IPVA

A major thread in our argument about the need to queer quantitative
stories of IPVA is our endorsement of a mixed-methods approach to
engage with the nuances of how violence, 'abusive' behaviours, power

and control operate in shifting and complex ways in LGB and/or T+ people's intimate relationships. Thus, we outline the result of our categorisation of the 36 qualitative accounts collected (see Chap. 2 for the selection criteria). As noted in Chap. 2, we coded each transcript independently using a coding framework that was both deductive, drawing on the characteristics of Johnson's (2008) typology, and inductive, leading us to develop new concepts such as experiential power and space for reaction, discussed next. Interview participants frequently discussed multiple relationships; hence, Table 4.1 includes accounts of over 50 relationships.

In the following case studies, we focus particularly on selected cases which, in different ways, problematise the notion of 'mutual abuse', and demonstrate both how participants enact space for reaction, and with what consequences.

Table 4.1 Categorisation of interview accounts

Category	Number of accounts	Interview participants
Clear evidence of perpetration	2	Adam, Brenda
Relationships where there are indications of controlling behaviour, but no dynamic of coercively controlling violence (CCV) or violent resistance (VR)	9	Amber, Clive, James, Jill, Judy, Leah, Lynn, Oscar, Owen
Separation-instigated violence	3	Harriet, Jill, Julie
Situational couple violence (SCV)	8	Adam, Amber, Angela, Harriet, James, Janet, Millie, Patricia
CCV victimisation	20	Adam, Alex, Amber, Amy, Beth, Clare, Colin, Graham, Harriet, Jack, Judy, Julie, Laura, Marceo, Marcus, Millie, Nicola, Patricia, Poppy, Ryan
Space for reaction: violent and/or non-violent resistance in response to CCV victimisation	8	Amy, Beth, Clare, Colin, Graham, Jack, Julie, Marcus, Millie, Ryan
No apparent experience or enactment of 'abusive' behaviours	7	Clive, Douglas, Eddie, Finn, Jane, Patrick, Paul[a]
Total number of accounts	57	

[a]Paul spoke about experiencing and enacting ostensibly 'abusive' behaviours in the context of consensual bondage, discipline, sadism and masochism (BDSM)

4.3   'Mutual Abuse'/Bidirectional Violence and a Reified Victim/Perpetrator Binary: Patricia's Story

Patricia's story exemplifies the problem highlighted by Messinger (2017, and discussed in Chap. 1) with much of the research on bidirectional violence: it is often assumed that the violent and 'abusive' behaviour reported within a study period was enacted within the same relationship. Patricia was a mixed heritage, cisgender lesbian in her late 40s who had been celibate for approximately 13 years prior to the interview. Before that she had been non-monogamous and had sex with 'at least 100 women', but she identified only six relationships that 'counted'. In her second relationship with Debbie, who was 'Caribbean', Patricia experienced identity abuse as a result of her 'race' and social class. Debbie called her a 'half-pig' for being mixed race, to 'definitely make it very clear that I wasn't full black, if there's such a thing'. Patricia did not call this racism but 'a level of discrimination or abuse around ethnicity'. Patricia identifies as middle class, and Debbie was working class. Debbie would say that she did not understand what Patricia was saying to her and 'banned' her from listening to a radio channel that she said was too middle class. Debbie also indiscriminately beat her:

> Nothing could trigger, do you see what I mean? I'd bought the wrong fish and I was beaten, what else? I couldn't fill in an insurance form and I was beaten, I didn't get up in time and I was beaten, so that was more about power.

Debbie was also into bondage, discipline, sadism and masochism (BDSM) and expected Patricia to comply against her will, once handcuffing Patricia to the bed and refusing to release her. Patricia said of Debbie and another violent lesbian partner, 'I think they preferred it, like you're the woman and I'm the man kind of thing'. On one occasion she managed to escape from Debbie and hide at the house of some friends, who went on Patricia's behalf and demanded Debbie give Patricia their baby daughter, whom Patricia was breastfeeding at the time. She describes the dilemma she had about not knowing where to get help to keep herself and her baby safe:

> [F]or maybe four or five years I lived in fear that me and the baby was going to die, there was nowhere I could go to, you couldn't go to Women's Aid [...] It was for [women abused by] men, what would they know about lesbian relationships? I think also you are stuck with that maybe this is your fault, you already know people don't think that lesbians should be together and here it is a woman's beating you.

Another time, the police became involved when Debbie 'must have forgot' that they had a male friend passenger in the car and did what she often 'used to do', which was to start beating her and then:

> [S]he'd say right, it's time to die now, and she would charge the car up and then slam on the brakes, so she's trying to, I don't know, there were just different ways of making me feel like I'm going to die.

Her friend went to the police, who visited Patricia at her workplace to see if she wanted to press charges, which she did not. Patricia explains how she felt after her doctor told her 'it's time you got out' when he was called to the house after a pregnant Patricia nearly lost her baby after a beating from Debbie:

> I don't know what was going on for me, I think it was really hard to leave— what I hadn't realised is how much Debbie had told my own friends lies so I become [sic] very isolated by this time.

Patricia explains that her lesbian friends did not know how to respond to her situation but certainly did not respond in the same way they might have had Patricia been in a relationship with a violent HC man: instead, they suggested that Patricia's behaviour was provocative. For example:

> [Her friend] said, 'Well, if Debbie's got two or three jobs and you're not doing anything what do you expect her'—I said, 'Pardon?', I says 'I actually work, I paid the mortgage, I pay this', so Debbie was already gone to my close friends and feed them things [...] so even lesbians question violence

or rape within relationships to the point that you're having to say, well, if I was straight and I was saying this you would take this automatically [...] [F]eminism doesn't look at relationships between women really.

In this relationship Patricia was clearly victimised by CCV: she lived in fear that she and her baby would be killed; she regularly had to hide; she was forced to have sex she did not want to have, including being restrained against her will; her male friend called the police because of his fear of what might be done to her and her partner told lies about her to their lesbian friends, which resulted in Patricia becoming increasingly isolated (see McDonald 2012), both from her lesbian friends and from feminism, to which she was, at the time, committed.

In talking about her use of violence, Patricia described being very violent for the only time in her life in one of her less serious relationships, towards a lover who, after they had had sex together, revealed that there had been another lover in the same sheets just hours before. Patricia explained that she had 'just let her have it', 'rammed her around the room', and then left to go to a lesbian centre, where she told them what she had done and said somebody should go and check on her lover. She says it was 'horrific', 'I think I was shocked, and I think I was concerned about her' and explains it by saying that she had realised she had rules, and that she did not want to sleep in the same sheets as another lover. She is candid about her violence, saying, 'That's the only woman I've ever picked my hand up to hit [...] but to be honest I didn't just pick my hand up and hit, I lost it'. She did not see the woman again and so did not know what happened to her.

In both of these relationships the violence was unidirectional, as was the coercive control by Debbie. Yet, in many studies on bidirectional violence, Patricia's experience would have been counted as bidirectional because of questions asking whether participants had experienced or enacted violence in a specified period of time, rather than in a specific relationship context. Patricia's account of victimisation and her own SCV also point to the instability of the victim/perpetrator binary and caution us to focus on the behaviours, direction of power, impacts and motives in a relationship context rather than on a type of person/perpetrator. Patricia acknowledges her potential to be violent and describes a time in her life when she had gone looking for a woman who had raped her with the intention of shooting her with a gun she had acquired for the purpose.

Interestingly, the unequal power dynamic in the relationship with Debbie was likened by Patricia to a heterosexual, cisgender (HC) one: she believed that Debbie wanted to be 'the man' and wanted Patricia to be 'the woman'. Donovan and Hester (2011, 2014) have argued that such sense-making derives from dominant heteronormative, and we would argue, cisnormative constructions of intimacy that produce a set of binaries about relationship roles such as decision-making and emotion work that map onto, but are not essentialist 'truths' about, cisgender heterosexual identities. They and others (Baker et al. 2013; Cannon et al. 2015; Hodes and Mennicke 2019) have argued that in navigating the debates about 'abusive' relationship dynamics, it is useful to unhook the behaviours of intimate partners from assumptions and expectations about embodied gender and sexuality identities in order to track the power dynamics of the relationship, identify the type of IPVA being enacted and experienced, and explore the motives and impacts, the heterogeneity of which was demonstrated in Chap. 3.

Like Stark (2012), we also argue that in making sense of IPVA, the relationship history and, indeed, each individual's relationship history (see Gadd and Corr 2017) are important. Everything that happens in the relationship as well as how it is understood is contingent on the social and cultural contexts within which the relationship is being lived; the intersecting identities of both partners; their friendship and family networks and relationships; their help-seeking practices; and their beliefs about love, marriage or civil partnership, sexuality, gender, intimacy and commitment (Barnes 2011; Donovan and Hester 2014). Decontextualised knowledge of someone's enactment of violence and 'abusive' behaviours should not lead to simplistic labelling of them as a 'perpetrator', nor should it assume that 'perpetrator' is a static identity.

The language used to describe the actors involved in IPVA is also crucial in reinforcing a particular construction of knowledge about it, especially in relation to mutual abuse. For example, whilst Messinger (2017) is critical of the lack of contextual knowledge elicited in many studies about bidirectional violence, making it unclear what kind of violence is being reported by participants and why, he nonetheless uses terminology that may reinforce a reified victim/perpetrator binary. His use of the term 'primary victim', which is meant to make a distinction about the use of IPVA in self-defence, for example, is helpful in distinguishing the partner who is most victimised; however, it also implies that the other partner might also sometimes be a victim, a secondary victim. Without being clear about the motives, intent and impacts of the IPVA, there is a danger that all IPVA is assumed to be the same. Terminology that keeps the terms 'victim' and 'perpetrator' central to the description of the relationship dynamic reinforces the binary; for example, Myhill (2017, p. 42) uses 'victims only, perpetrators only or victim-perpetrators within a given relationship'. The terms 'victim' and 'perpetrator' are value-laden, implying that the actor who perpetrates violence should only and always be understood in the same way and conversely that victims constitute a homogenous group. Certainly, in law not all violence is understood to be 'the same', and context and motives are taken into account during prosecution and sentencing. It follows that in other areas of practice language should be carefully chosen so that those who have used space for reaction and used physical or non-physical VR in response to CCV will not be wary about coming forward for help for fear that they will be treated as a perpetrator.

4.4   Barriers to Recognition of Victimisation— the Victim/Perpetrator Binary: Marcus' Story

For several interview participants, the victim/perpetrator binary prevented them from understanding their own domestic violence and abuse (DVA) victimisation. Guadalupe-Diaz and Jasinski (2017) explain that their transgender participants rejected a victim identity because it was one they equated with hyper-femininity and passivity, which seemed incongruous with their deployment of help-seeking strategies or their own use of physical violence in self-defence. The binaries of male/female, victim/perpetrator in the public story of DVA reinforce the construction of an ideal victim/survivor who is defenceless and blameless (Christie

1986), which makes those victimised susceptible to a range of victim-blaming beliefs about their provocation of IPVA. At the same time, Donovan and Hester (2014) argue that the self-perception of those victimised is constructed through the relationship rule that they are the responsible and agentic partners in the relationship, which mitigates against a self-perception of being passive or blameless. Indeed, victimised partners in their study often identified as the emotionally stronger partner in the relationship, which resulted in many rejecting the idea that they were a 'victim' of DVA (Donovan and Hester 2014). However, what the relationship rules do not take account of are the times when victimised partners use IPVA themselves in reaction to their abusive partner by physically or non-physically (e.g. verbally) fighting back, defending themselves, their children, their property, their friends and/or family, retaliating, seeking revenge or in other ways attempting to rebalance the relationship to make it more equal or 'levelling the playing field' (see Velonis 2016, p. 1046). The next case study illustrates how the ideal victim/perpetrator binary provides additional barriers to recognising victimisation.

The account of Marcus, a white transgender man in his early 20s who identifies as queer/pansexual, illustrates this point. His first serious relationship which started when he was 16 years old was with a lesbian, Thea, who was five years older than him. This was before he transitioned and identified as a lesbian. Marcus was estranged from his family of origin, living in supported housing and unemployed. Thea was living with and supported by her family, and Marcus spent a lot of time there, enjoying what he experienced as a much more loving and supportive family. He was financially dependent on Thea, which meant he 'wasn't really in a position to say anything'. Later in the relationship, Thea 'made me feel like I was lucky to be with her'. Thea was also a leading light in the local LGBT+ scene, and Marcus explained how being in a relationship with her 'gave me status'.

Marcus also explains that he was very unhappy as a young teenager, which, with hindsight, he attributes to his transitioning journey and a serious accident that had left him with mental health problems; he also used drugs and self-harmed. His partner made clear on numerous occasions that having sex with men was 'horrible', which made it difficult for

Marcus to identify in any other way than as a lesbian or to reflect on his gender identity. The relationship rules (Donovan and Hester 2014) were established: Thea was 'the decision-maker'; she controlled the finances and controlled Marcus' time—when she would see him and what they would do. He says, 'I'd feel really anxious and upset' if he was late, if Thea did not call, or if he thought she was angry with him. At first Marcus felt 'grateful' that Thea wanted to spend time with him, 'appreciating' her attention and 'feeling secure and feeling part of something'. He loved Thea but gradually lost his sense of self: 'I wore her clothes and did things that she thought was good and attractive. [...] I followed her lead. [...] I let her construct me as a person'. He felt he needed 'permission' from Thea 'for everything'. Whilst Thea never said no to Marcus doing his own things, he would feel guilty because he knew she did not like 'feeling excluded', but equally she did not like his friends or his family. Thus, he became isolated from both. Sexually, Thea also took control, demanding more than once that Marcus and she have 'make-up sex', 'to keep the peace'. This 'smashed up' Marcus' trust in Thea, whereas earlier on in the relationship, he had felt sexually liberated.

Looking back, Marcus says the relationship was 'really, really stormy, really quite dark at times'. He also says that at the time he was very much in love with Thea and explained away her controlling ways, believing that she did not mean to control him. It is only with hindsight that he wonders whether 'she possibly, in a way, did'. When Marcus is asked whether he experienced DVA, he says no. He explains that he was not 'easy to be with', that he believes Thea started self-harming only because of him, and that things would not have been as bad if he had been a 'sound mind, sound body'. He recognises that the relationship had 'very dangerous elements to it', but also that he 'was never like a battered wife'. He explains how, over time, he began to resent being controlled by Thea, that they began to row and 'at points [we] got quite aggressive about it as well. [...] We were just as bad as each other, we were fiery, really fiery', shouting, swearing, name-calling and 'intentionally being horrible to each other'. Occasionally it became physical. Marcus finds this difficult to talk about, in part because 'I've never really been that person'. They would grab each other's arms, push, 'throw against a wall'; yet, he says, 'I never bruised her, like I never had bruises'. His love for Thea also meant that he could not leave her: 'She was quite aggressive [...] but I could never imagine walking away from her. [...] I didn't really have that option'.

Marcus, in making sense of his relationship, cannot find himself in the public story of DVA, for several reasons. The relationship was not an HC one, and Thea's physical violence was neither frequent nor unidirectional: he was not, as he puts it, a 'battered wife'. However, it is possible to read his use of the term 'battered wife' not only in terms of physical violence but also in terms of being cowed, physically and mentally. His reflection on gender roles within this relationship, within a heteronormative framework, reinforces how he made sense of this relationship: during the interview he reflected on how speaking about it was making him think about a book he was currently reading about power, control and abusive men. He says that in terms of being the man in the relationship, 'it definitely was not me'.

Marcus did not present himself as a victim either: he wanted to explain how he could become angry, frustrated, resentful towards Thea—all evidence of using space for reaction, his physical and non-physical resistance to Thea's coercive control. He was unhappy in the relationship but attributed this to his own problems. Indeed, he felt that Thea's problems were of his making. Some of this is victim-blaming, a very common feature of those being victimised in DVA. However, some of this is not recognising victimisation, because the evidence of his own experience suggests that there is no blamelessness and no defencelessness. In the survey, Marcus provides his reasons for his use of behaviours: to protect yourself from them; to retaliate against them; because of your emotional problems; because you were unhappy in the relationship; because you were unhappy in work/life. This profile of reasons is brought to life in the interview. None of his reasons are self-serving, but they also include retaliation. Marcus is not passive; he does not accept the ways things are. He creates space for reaction. However, using space for reaction is limited in its positive effect because it takes place within a coercively controlling relationship.

Marcus was structurally (age, employment, housing, financially) and emotionally dependent on Thea; she wielded experiential power over him because of her status in the local LGBT scene. The impacts are far-ranging: loss of self-esteem and self-confidence; increased anxiety and exacerbation of his mental health problems and substance use; losing trust, becoming isolated. Because he loved her, he did not feel he had the option to leave (Donovan and Hester 2014). All of these behaviours are indicative of victimisation and particularly reflect the impacts of a constellation of coercively controlling behaviours that limited Marcus' space for action (Kelly 2003; Wilcox 2006). In quantitative surveys his behaviours or relationship might be categorised as mutual abuse. However, his qualitative account is of a situationally vulnerable young adult being coercively controlled by a much better resourced, older, cisgender lesbian, against whom Marcus occasionally enacted non-physical and physical VR in order to (re)establish some equality in the relationship.

4.5 Patriarchal Influences in the Relationships of LGB and/or T+ People: Colin's Story

Threaded through Patricia's and Marcus' sense-making of their relationships have been heteronormative, cisnormative assumptions about the constructions of adult intimacy. Their accounts indicate their beliefs and/or expectations that a heteronormative, cisnormative binary of relationship roles/norms that map onto male/female, victim/perpetrator binaries provides a template for understanding the abuse of power that took place in their own relationships. Colin's account illustrates a different aspect of these beliefs and expectations. Colin, a white, cisgender gay man in his mid-30s, came out when he was 30 years old, having never experienced any adult intimate or sexual relationship, having no LGB and/or T+ friends that he was aware of, and no knowledge of LGB and/or T+ lives. Where he lived did not have a visible LGBT scene. His first gay relationship was with a man who was ten years younger than him, who had been out for approximately five years and had had several gay relationships before Colin. Colin explains that with hindsight he can see that the relationship developed unduly quickly because when he met Nathan at the age of 32:

> [I] kind of tried to make up for lost time, and when I'd found somebody that I thought was the one, everything just was all systems go, hundred

mile an hour. He stayed over on the first night that we got together. He stayed over the second night. Went home to his parents on the third night, and then by the fourth night he'd moved in.

Colin was already established in his career and had his own home, two markers of being structurally and materially secure. Nathan had neither, had lived with his family until he moved in with Colin, and had insecure low-paid work. On the face of it, this positions Nathan as structurally subordinate to Colin. However, Colin was in love, and had no knowledge about what being gay might be like. Nathan, having been out for longer, was very quickly able, in part by exerting experiential power, to establish the relationship rules (Donovan and Hester 2014) that he was the key decision-maker about the relationship and Colin was responsible for him. Whilst Colin wanted to 'get married and settle down', believing that he and Nathan could be together forever, Nathan would undermine him, saying:

> You don't have a clue. You don't know how the LGBT community works. That's not real life. You're living in some kind of straight utopia. That's not the way that it works and that's not the way that the scene works'. It was, 'you've got a lot to learn. You've got a lot to be aware of'.

Colin financially subsidised Nathan and accrued £10,000 of debt by the end of their one-year relationship, partly because an element of Nathan's control involved expecting Colin to pay for him or to buy him things as an exchange for his affection and/or time, and sometimes for sex. Colin used space for reaction to argue against unnecessary expenditure but Nathan would keep asking until Colin capitulated:

> 'Well, I don't want to upset you, and I don't want to put you in a bad mood. So let's just get them and put them on the credit card. That'll be fine'. That would happen on kind of a regular basis.

Nathan was able to coerce Colin into submitting to his demands by playing on Colin's insecurities about his physical attractiveness, thus reinforcing fears that he would be unable to find another partner:

I was so insecure and so vulnerable. And the way that he would manipulate me and the way that he would make me feel, almost as though I should be grateful that he was with me, and because my mindset was, again, I like the younger guys, so therefore what have I got to offer? I'm not really that physically attractive. I'm a little bit overweight. I'm receding. […] He knew that that was a weakness, and he would play on that.

Colin also felt unable to challenge Nathan's behaviour because about three weeks after having moved in, Nathan, during a night of heavy drinking, revealed that he had been sexually abused as a child by a family friend. Colin believed that Nathan's behaviour was a result of his having been abused, and he thought that because he loved Nathan, he could support him to come to terms with what had happened. Thus, Nathan's neediness elicited Colin's love and care (Donovan and Hester 2014) and the impact was profound:

That kind of set the scene from there on in where I felt as though I was treading on eggshells, because I knew that he'd had this past, and I didn't really know how to deal with it, because I'd never been in that situation myself. It was a case of, 'Well, I just need to give you whatever you need'.

It is in this coercively controlling relationship context that Colin explains that about every month, things would come to a head between them, usually after their both drinking heavily. Nathan would become 'nasty and vindictive':

[He] knew exactly all of the things that would upset me, you know, calling me things like a dirty old pervert and, you know, not good enough and not worthy and, desperate and all these kind of things. All the things that would really kind of upset me and, 'I will ruin you. I'll ruin your career', all that kind of thing.

Nathan's threats to out Colin in his job and positioning of Colin as a sexual predator exacerbated the rows, which would, eventually, become physical 'brawls' where Colin would 'throw a punch', after which he would apologise and be ashamed of himself.

Reflecting on why he might have responded with physical violence in the altercations with Nathan, Colin reflects on his socialisation as an ostensibly HC man. He did not speak to anybody at the time about what was going on in the relationship, and believes:

> Coming from sort of a heterosexual background, and the whole kind of male testosterone-filled, you know, two blokes having a little bit of an argy-bargy, it's just kind of acceptable. [...] I didn't necessarily see that as being a problem at the time. It was just he's pushed me too far and it's become physical. [...] If one of my friends had kind of had a go at me and wound me up as well, then I'd probably throw a punch at them as well, or they would throw a punch at me. So it's the kind of the, the male thing to do.

Colin also critiques this understanding and explains that 'when you look at it in the context of a relationship, it's totally, totally different'; yet his sense of what might be normalised in some cultural contexts as acceptable—an aggressive heteronormative, cisnormative masculinity in response to disagreement or conflict—provides some insight into the ways in which patriarchal factors shape how heterosexual and gay men might treat each other, both inside and outside of intimate relationships. Thus, patriarchal norms can make it difficult for men like Colin to problematise their own behaviour as well as to recognise their experiences as being contextualised in a coercively controlling relationship, which, in turn, can affect help-seeking. Colin, at the time, normalised his response whilst feeling ashamed after each incident. He was able to problematise the physical violence in his relationship, including his own use of physical violence, but could not recognise his experiences as DVA. He could talk about Nathan being 'controlling' and 'manipulative', but he put this down to Nathan having been abused:

> As far as I was concerned, everything could be attributed to his abusive past. And everything that he was doing, all of his behaviours, was as a result of that [...] if I wanted to be with him, then that was part of the package. I had to deal with that. And [I did] because I did love him so much.

Love, as Donovan and Hester (2011, 2014) have shown, can be especially important in making sense of how DVA relationship dynamics work (see also Fraser 2008; Lloyd and Emery 2000). Whilst the abusive partner establishes the relationship rules, in ways reminiscent of what is expected of HC masculinity in a heterosexual DVA relationship, they also reveal their emotional neediness in a way that elicits care, love and support from the victimised partner—a characteristic associated with HC femininity. Thus, straightforward gendered binaries are actually not easily identified in many DVA relationships (Donovan and Hester 2014). In Colin's case, his love for Nathan, as well as his fears about finding another partner, were part of the constellation of factors that restricted his space for action. Nevertheless, Colin also created space for reaction when he regularly used verbal and physical resistance, retaliation and revenge in response to Nathan's verbal threats and abuse.

Colin's account as recorded in a survey exploring mutual abuse and directionality, including a question about who initiated the physical violence, would likely count Colin as a perpetrator or the relationship as one characterised by mutual abuse. In our survey he falls into the category of high perpetration (see Chap. 3). Yet, his qualitative account makes clear that Colin was being coercively controlled by Nathan, with impacts for his self-esteem, anxiety about his body image and age and his ability to be loved; fears about his employment; of being left alone and lonely; and his identity as an authentic gay man. His use of space for reaction with regular acts of verbal and physical violence, often in an attempt to stop Nathan's taunting and tormenting of him but also in some situations in retaliation and revenge, can be read as Colin resisting the control of his partner and re-establishing his own sense of identity as a person who might be respected.

The motives Colin reported in the survey for his use of violent and 'abusive' behaviour were as follows: because they hit you first; to protect yourself from them; to retaliate against them; to prevent them harming themselves; because you didn't trust them; because you were unhappy in the relationship; didn't feel good enough/felt insecure; because you didn't know what else to do. As Velonis (2016) suggests in her qualitative study of HC women who fought back against their violent and abusive HC male partners, Colin's response can be seen as 'a reactive response to ongoing attacks on self-worth and autonomy'; they are attempts to 'reclaim lost control', but in a coercively controlling relationship the partner victimised is 'constantly at a loss' (Velonis 2016, p. 1050); thus, they regularly engage in space for reaction.

4.6 Resistance as Demeanour: Clare's Story

The problem with using concepts such as 'resistance' (whether physically violent or not) is that they are often operationalised in ways that reflect the tradition of focussing on incidents of IPVA rather than a relationship context and history, or on a demeanour responding to relationship conditions. With Clare's account, we unpack the term 'resistance' to illustrate why asking survey respondents to indicate their motives for violence enacted should be done with caution.

Emerging research (Cannon et al. 2015; Hamby 2009) that explores motives of HC women and men for their use of IPVA produces knowledge about anger, frustration, and/or retaliation, that are typically understood in incident-based ways. Yet, in our work it became clear that resistance to CCV is not confined to particular instances but can become a full-time response to the relationship. Clare is a white, bisexual, cisgender woman in her 30s who, during her twenties, was in a relationship of six years with Emma. Emma was opposed to 'giving your money to the banks' and insisted on only using cash. Clare described her as 'a proper dodgy character', constantly involved with various 'scams'—for example, claiming state benefits whilst still working; and never paying for things 'properly', because she always knew somebody who could do it cheaper. Clare learned to leave things to Emma, but this also meant that Clare was never registered as living in the house, so that they would not have to pay council tax for her, and consequently she could not vote. At first she went along with Emma being in charge of all the finances, even though this meant that Emma gradually also became the decision-maker about how money was spent. Thus, relationship rules (Donovan and Hester 2014) were beginning to be established in material ways. The arguments started in relation to Emma's insecurities about Clare's friends and ex-lovers, as she explains:

> I sort of went into the relationship wanting to discuss things […] but very quickly she got very, very insecure about sort of past, immediate, informal

relationships that I was having or had. [...] So things like works dos, one of the past relationships was with somebody at work, so any work do I went to [...] within half an hour I'd just be receiving texts, 'so they're there? I bet they are [freaked out noise]', and in the end [...] I'd go home. Um and then I just stopped going out, so I was quite submissive I guess in that sense, and that really annoyed me.

Emma's neediness in relation to her insecurity makes it Clare's responsibility (the second relationship rule) to reassure her about her fidelity. Verbal reassurance is not enough, so Clare stops going out without Emma. However, what is interesting to note is that as Clare becomes isolated she adopts not a passive, defenceless ideal victim mentality, but a more *agentic* response: she is annoyed and instead of becoming a meek obedient partner, she finds space for reaction and attempts to reassert an equal balance in the relationship. She explains what happened to her own character as a result of Emma's behaviour:

In my six-year relationship [...] I saw a really scary change in me. I'm a very gentle person[...] but [...] after the first year I found myself getting really aggressive and, you know, one of the only ways I could meet or communicate with Emma was, was by climbing that ladder, by escalating that shouting match, [and] that kind of got worse.

Clare's attempts to meet Emma's verbal abuse were not successful: as she says, it got worse. Alongside this, Emma was enacting identity abuse by trying to make Clare more femme; she started buying Clare clothes and expecting her to behave in certain ways that reflected Emma's other lesbian friends, who were also in butch/femme relationships. Clare had already realised that being bisexual was not acceptable in Emma's eyes, so identified as a lesbian in this relationship. However, she resisted Emma's attempts to get her to perform a more feminine presentation of self, and this was, over time, detrimental to Clare's own sense of self. Clare explains her non-physical resistance to these attempts at micro-managing and coercively controlling her dress, hairstyle and behaviours:

Because you've got this control situation going on, I felt that becoming more femme was being submissive and [...] you're kind of buying into this whole kind of 'okay, honey, yeah, I'll let you pay for that' and 'I'll just keep quiet over here while you go and talk about bikes and stuff', 'I'll make the tea'. [...] I didn't want to do that. I sort of wanted to feel like I was on an equal footing, which [led to] the change in the way I was dressing myself, and trying to find that piece in me that maybe was a little bit more masculine.

Such agency and employment of space for reaction on the part of Clare are probably part of the reason she did not problematise her relationship with Emma beyond its being 'controlling'. She believes she endeavoured to put the relationship back on an 'equal footing' by her resistant stance. When she talked about their sexual relationship—which was Clare's first with another woman—she describes Emma as saying things like 'is that the best you can do?' and that Clare 'fuck[ed] like a straight woman', which made Clare feel insecure. The fact that this was Clare's first relationship enabled Emma to exert experiential power (Donovan and Barnes in press; Donovan et al. 2014); it can also be read as biphobic identity abuse. Yet, Clare maintains that she was, at least initially, able to explore herself sexually, because of Emma's openness to sex. What is also apparent in Clare's account are the impacts of living in a small town in which there is little visible LGBT scene and the resulting small subcultures of LGB and/or T+ life that create norms of being that are difficult to resist (Hassouneh and Glass 2008). The isolation Clare felt was exacerbated by Emma's friends, whose adherence to a butch/femme subculture was alien to her. Whilst performance of butch/femme identities has no correlation with IPVA (Barnes 2013; Ristock 2002; Donovan and Hester 2014), Emma used it to legitimise her controlling behaviours.

Whilst Clare acknowledges Emma's control over her, she does not recognise herself as having been a victim of DVA. She describes arguments in which Emma raised her fist on several occasions, and once 'she'd sort of, it wasn't necessarily a punch, it was like a slow push with a fist that sent me to the floor'. In her explanation it becomes clear what the term 'arguments' meant in the context of their relationship:

She would, she'd follow me round the house, she was like just digging, just she would find something to dig into, um. It's like a nipping, it wasn't shouting, it was accusative, almost like verbal pokes, you know, 'and you don't do this, and I bet you want', you know, 'I bet you do that' and [sighs].

Clare balances her account of the relationship and describes an occasion when she was physically violent towards Emma:

I remember getting really frustrated and, you know, this kind of [...] verbal poking ended up in me turning round and just saying, 'Look I've had enough, you know, I've really had enough of this', and by then [...] [laughs] you're like that in each other's faces. [...] She pushed me in the shoulders, turned around and walked off, yeah, and I, I sort of shoved her in the back. 'You don't walk away from me, I'm talking to you', shove. She fell and came this close to smacking her head on the loo, and [...] it was that, that really [clicks fingers] sort of hit home that something had to stop, something had to change.

Clare problematises her own behaviour, and that became the catalyst for change. She does not recognise her experience as DVA, but as a relationship that transformed her into somebody she did not particularly like. Yet, her description of the impact of the relationship on her crystallises her victimisation:

I think that relationship has taught me [...] the possibility of the way, if you allow it, somebody else can really kind of drag you down, whether it's emotionally, physically. [...] I just completely lost my sense of self-respect [...] Yeah, just felt really lost for a long time. I remember looking in the mirror [...] and just not recognising who was looking back at me. Like I say, like my hair was shorter, I'd gained four stone, and I was dressing in clothes that I'd never have dreamt of dressing in.

These are the impacts Johnson (2008) and others (e.g. Kelly and Johnson 2008; Stark and Hester 2019) have identified as characteristic of those being victimised by CCV: loss of self and self-esteem and damaging coping mechanisms such as excessive weight gain. In the final year of their relationship, Clare withdrew emotionally and sexually from Emma. Her resistance was successful insofar as Emma quite quickly acted on her threat that if Clare was 'not going to put out [she would] go and get it somewhere else', and she started a new relationship before Clare had moved out. Clare's account reported in a survey could be read as 'mutual abuse'. Yet, Emma's micro-regulation of Clare's everyday life through her financial control, identity abuse, exertion of experiential power, isolation and accusatory behaviours reflects Stark's coercive control, which, he explains, 'includes multiple tactics in addition to violence; and emphasises harms to autonomy, personhood and basic rights as well as to physical security' (Stark 2010, p. 201). Clare's account also illustrates how, as Lempert (1997, p. 291) puts it, 'as "victims" they are not entirely passive and as "agents" they are not co-acting as equals in their interactions with their [...] partners'. Even whilst Clare recognises the control she is subject to and creates spaces for reaction, because this is done within a relationship of DVA, her capacity for truly redressing the power balance is limited and, takes its toll on her.

4.7　A Planned Resistance: Amy's Story

Amy's experience also illustrates how a demeanour of resistance can be not only non-physically violent and consciously agentic, but also consciously self-protective. A key difference in Amy's story is that she plans early on how she is going to manage leaving the relationship safely. Amy, a white, cisgender lesbian, aged 19 years, had her first lesbian relationship with a cisgender woman who was of similar age to her, whom she met through college. Amy calls this partner 'Voldemort' after the arch-enemy character in the Harry Potter novels, because it encapsulated how Amy thought about her: 'she who must not be named [laughs], I can't stand her name, it makes my skin crawl'. In their eight-month relationship, Amy describes Voldemort as a 'manipulative liar' who was 'obsessive'. The obsession became clear after a month of being together, when Voldemort proposed to Amy, and after the relationship ended, when Voldemort stalked her for two years. Some of Voldemort's lies seemed inconsequential (e.g. claiming to have a job), whilst others had a more profound impact on Amy's life, such as Voldemort claiming to be allergic to nuts, which for Amy as a vegan meant the she 'had to kind of really change the way entirely how I was living'.

Amy also recounts that on several occasions when they were arguing, Voldemort would block Amy's bedroom door so that she could not walk out. There were signs of sexual abuse as well; for example, Amy woke in the night to Voldemort 'groping' her, sometimes not stopping when Amy asked her, which 'frightened' her. Her partner was also sexually inappropriate in public, expecting Amy to respond to what she experienced as inappropriate touching, hugging and kissing. Voldemort slapped Amy around the face a couple of times and 'manhandled' her in public. She also tried to mould Amy's dress style and make-up. As Amy explains:

> She would complain if I would wear more make-up than usual, or if, for a change, I'd wear heels. [...] She would be unhappy with that and would say, you know, 'I would like you to go and wear something else', or like 'if your skirt was longer' or whatever, and it'd be like 'go away, I'll dress how I want, it's my body'.

In explanation of Voldemort's behaviour, Amy felt that she 'kind of had it in her mind that she was the man in the relationship. [...] She'd kind of decided that that was her role and she would speak to me like that [...] demeaningly'. Again, Amy draws on a heteronormative, cisnormative construction of an abusive HC relationship to make sense of her partner's behaviours. For several reasons Amy is able to call this relationship controlling, but not DVA. Her ability to create space for reaction and use non-physical VR was one. Her response to being expected to wear particular clothes and being criticised for her use of make-up led her to reassert her own presentation of self: 'I would often go further out of my way to irritate her [...] the skirts would get shorter, the make-up would be more. I would just do it to irritate her'.

The second reason is another aspect of her resistance, which shows more foresight and planning about how to end the relationship and when to do it safely. The relationship had started at the beginning of the college year in September, and by the end of October she had decided that this relationship had to end; however, she calculated that she should not end it until the end of the academic year:

> I [...] knew she was going to be in my class for the rest of the year, and I thought 'I don't want to have to deal with breaking up with you in like the

October and having to deal with you until June'. [...] [I] broke up with her in April, I think, or May, um so I didn't have to really tolerate her behaving strangely in college for too long, cos the term finished in June, but it was long enough to be very uncomfortable.

This self-protective decision about when to end the relationship did not work. Amy was stalked for two years by Voldemort, and had to change her mobile number, her routes to and from college, and where and when she socialised. She showed further agency by talking to the college about Voldemort's stalking of her but was offered a mediated discussion between the two of them, which she refused. She became isolated in college because, as Patricia also recounted, Voldemort had successfully positioned herself as the victim in the situation, which resulted in mutual friends being judgemental of Amy and continuing to talk to her about Voldemort. She did not keep any of the mobile and e-mail messages Voldemort sent her and had felt this meant she could not go to the police, even though she had been 'terrified'. Amy still did not see this as an abusive relationship, because she focussed on the physical violence and explained them as 'isolated incidents':

Voldemort could be a bit sharp with me, and obviously hitting me across the face wasn't very nice, but I don't think the relationship as a whole was abusive, I think these were kind of like isolated incidents that happened towards the end.

Lloyd and Emery (2000) found evidence of this isolating and separating off of violent incidents in their qualitative exploration of physical and sexual aggression in the relationships of HC women. They argue that this allows HC women to maintain a relationship narrative that is not one of violence and abuse. Whilst Amy seems to adopt a similar approach and isolates the experience of physical violence into separate incidents, she is not doing so in order to defend or remain in the relationship, but to reject the idea that the relationship constituted DVA. Because her strategy had been from early on that she needed to leave the relationship, she believed herself to be resisting control rather than being cowed by it.

The public story of DVA, which prioritises physical violence, is crucial here in shaping how Amy makes sense of her experiences. However, her account also illustrates a problem with typologies that unintentionally create 'ideal types' that restrict DVA to the most extreme form in which all space for action and reaction has been lost. Amy was clearly being victimised by a coercively controlling and violent (ex)partner; yet, even after two years of being stalked, and still having to take account of Voldemort at college, Amy did not understand herself to be entrapped or without agency and remained able to create spaces for reaction both whilst she was in the relationship and afterwards.

4.8   Summary

In this chapter we have drawn on five case studies of participants who were selected to be interviewed because they reported IPVA perpetration in the survey to make two points. First is to queer the assumptions made that the relationships of LGB and/or T+ people are free of heternormative and/or cisnormative roles and/or norms. Second is to suggest that space for reaction provides a way of accounting for some of the behaviours that might otherwise be uncritically reported in quantitative research and in practice as mutual abuse or bidirectional violence.

We argue that three key assumptions are made in relation to DVA in the relationships of LGB and/or T+ people: (i) that these relationships are free of gender inequalities, both partners are 'the same' and therefore any IPVA occurring is between 'equals', not risky or harmful; (ii) either, because unequal cisnormative, heteronormative gender roles are not operating, any IPVA that occurs is mutual abuse; (iii) or, in order to establish who the perpetrator and victim are, the partner whose presentation of gender is more 'like a HC man' can be assumed to be the perpetrator and the partner whose presentation of gender is 'more like a HC woman' can be assumed to be the victim.

Participants' sense-making gives the lie to the belief that the relationships of LGB and/or T+ people are gender- or patriarchy-free. Colin's account of his violence refers back to his understanding of being socialised into heteronormative, cisnormative masculinity that normalises physical violence between HC men as a way of responding to conflict. In their accounts, there appear to be three layers to the comparisons Patricia,

Marcus, Clare and Amy make with the public story of DVA. The first leads them to conclude that their abusive partner was behaving 'like a man'. The second leads them to minimise their experiences because they deem them to be not as bad as 'the battered woman', that is, not characterised by extreme physical violence. The third is shaped by beliefs about the ideal victim characterised by the battered woman: that she is defenceless and blameless. Their use of space for reaction in enacting IPVA whether physical or non-physical leads them to assume they have not been victimised. The implications of this for help-seeking are explored in Chap. 5.

We also suggest space for reaction as a way of describing the IPVA used by participants in response to their partners' DVA. Space for reaction provides a better way of understanding the behaviours of victimised partners and unpacking simplistic assumptions about mutual abuse. The case studies indicate the extent to which victimised partners underestimate the power dynamics that are unfolding in their relationships, and the extent to which they are, despite their best efforts, being coercively controlled with physical and non-physical violence. The relationship rules, whilst providing an explanation for why many of those victimised by DVA do not recognise themselves as victimised because they feel agentic, responsible and managing their relationship (Donovan and Hester 2014), do not account for those who utilise space for reaction. By asking about what participants do, rather than only what they experience, it is clear that they often resist and/or fight back. However, resistance and/or fighting back are not necessarily or only incident-specific and we point to the relationship demeanour that can emerge when those victimised utilise space for reaction to struggle to reassert their own integrity in the relationship and a more equal power relationship. In Chap. 5 we provide a visual representation of space for reaction via the Coral Project Power, Control and Space for Reaction Wheel (adapted from Donovan and Hester 2014), which we offer for use in practice settings.

Finally, we have queried the term 'mutual abuse' for being too easily applied to the relationships of LGB and/or T+ people as well as to query the implications for help-seeking of the reification of the victim/perpetrator binary. As we discuss in the next chapter, most do not seek any formal sources of help, perhaps because, like Marcus, those victimised position themselves as having been to blame. Whilst not condoning the use of IPVA, we argue that there is a case for practitioners' careful assessment of whether and how power and control are operating in the relationship context, informed by Johnson's typology and those who have built on this (see Chap. 1), in order to ensure that their responses are tailored and appropriate.

References

Baker, N. L., Buick, J. D., Kim, S. R., Moniz, S., & Nava, K. L. (2013). Lessons from examining same-sex intimate partner violence. *Sex Roles: A Journal of Research, 69*(3–4), 182–192.

Barnes, R. (2011). 'Suffering in a silent vacuum': Woman-to-woman partner abuse as a challenge to the lesbian feminist vision. *Feminism & Psychology, 21*(2), 233–239.

Barnes, R. (2013). 'She expected her women to be pretty, subservient, dinner on the table at six': Problematising the narrative of egalitarianism in lesbian relationships through accounts of woman-to-woman partner abuse. In T. Sanger & Y. Taylor (Eds), *Mapping intimacies: Relations, exchanges, affects* (pp. 130–149). Basingstoke: Palgrave Macmillan.

Cannon, C., Lauve-Moon, K., & Buttell, F. (2015). Re-theorizing intimate partner violence through post-structural feminism, queer theory, and sociology of gender. *Social Sciences, 4*, 668–687.

Christie, N. (1986). The ideal victim. In E. Fattah (Ed.), *From crime policy to victim policy: Reorienting the justice system* (pp. 17–30). Basingstoke: Macmillan.

Donovan, C., & Barnes, R. (in press). Help-seeking among lesbian, gay, bisexual and/or transgender victims/survivors of domestic violence and abuse: The impacts of cisgendered heteronormativity and invisibility. *Journal of Sociology.* https://doi.org/10.1177/1440783319882088

Donovan, C., Barnes, R., & Nixon, C. (2014). *The Coral Project: Exploring abusive behaviours in lesbian, gay, bisexual and/or transgender relationships: Interim report.* Sunderland and Leicester: University of Sunderland and University of Leicester. Retrieved March 30, 2019, from https://www2.le.ac.uk/departments/criminology/documents/coral-project-interim-report

Donovan, C., & Hester, M. (2011). Exploring emotion work in domestically abusive relationships. In J. Ristock (Ed.), *Intimate partner violence in LGBTQ lives* (pp. 81–101). New York and Abingdon: Routledge.

Donovan, C., & Hester, M. (2014). *Domestic violence and sexuality: What's love got to do with it?* Bristol: Policy Press.

Fraser, H. (2008). *In the name of love: Women's narratives of love and abuse.* Toronto: Women's Press, an imprint of Canadian Scholars' Press Inc.

Gadd, D., & Corr, M. (2017). Beyond typologies: Foregrounding meaning and motive in domestic violence perpetration. *Deviant Behavior, 38*(7), 781–791.

Guadalupe-Diaz, X. L., & Jasinski, J. (2017). 'I wasn't a priority, I wasn't a victim': Challenges in help seeking for transgender survivors of intimate partner violence. *Violence Against Women, 23*(6), 772–792.

Hamby, S. (2009). The gender debate about intimate partner violence: Solutions and dead ends. *Psychological Trauma: Theory, Research, Practice, and Policy, 1*(1), 24–34.

Hassouneh, D., & Glass, N. (2008). The influence of gender role stereotyping on women's experiences of female same-sex intimate partner violence. *Violence Against Women, 14*(3), 310–325.

Hodes, C., & Mennicke, A. (2019). Is it conflict or abuse? A practice note for furthering differential assessment and response. *Journal of Clinical Social Work, 47*(2), 176–184.

Johnson, M. P. (2008). *A typology of domestic violence: Intimate terrorism, violent resistance, and situational couple violence.* Boston: Northeastern University Press.

Kelly, J. B., & Johnson, M. P. (2008). Differentiation among types of intimate partner violence: Research update and implications for interventions. *Family Court Review, 46*(3), 476–499.

Kelly, L. (2003). The wrong debate: Reflections on why force is not the key issue with respect to trafficking in women for sexual exploitation. *Feminist Review, 73*, 139–144.

Lempert, L. (1997). The other side of help: Negative effects in the help-seeking processes of abused women. *Qualitative Sociology, 20*(2), 289–309.

Lloyd, S., & Emery, B. (2000). *The dark side of courtship: Physical and sexual aggression.* London: Sage.

McDonald, C. (2012). The social context of woman-to-woman intimate partner abuse (WWIPA). *Journal of Family Violence, 27*(7), 635–645.

Messinger, A. M. (2017). *LGBTQ intimate partner violence: Lessons for policy, practice, and research.* Oakland, CA: University of California Press.

Myhill, A. (2017). Measuring domestic violence: Context is everything. *Journal of Gender-Based Violence, 1*, 33–44.

Ristock, J. (2002). *No more secrets: Violence in lesbian relationships.* London and New York: Routledge.

Stark, E. (2010). Do violent acts equal abuse? Resolving the gender parity/asymmetry dilemma. *Sex Roles, 62,* 201–211.

Stark, E. (2012). Looking beyond domestic violence: Policing coercive control. *Journal of Police Crisis Negotiations, 12,* 199–217.

Stark, E., & Hester, M. (2019). Coercive control: Update and review. *Violence Against Women, 25*(1), 81–104.

Velonis, A. J. (2016). He never did anything you typically think of as abuse: Experiences with violence in controlling and non-controlling relationships in a non-agency sample of women. *Violence Against Women, 22*(9), 1031–1054.

Wilcox, P. (2006). *Surviving domestic violence: Gender, poverty and agency.* Basingstoke: Palgrave Macmillan.

5

Hearing a New Story About Intimate Partner Violence and Abuse

Abstract In Chapter 5, our focus shifts to the implications of our findings for policy and practice. We begin with a brief overview of current policy and practice responses to both LGB and/or T+ intimate partner violence and abuse (IPVA) and perpetrators of domestic violence and abuse (DVA) within the UK, with significant gaps in provision for all perpetrators being noted. However, we demonstrate in this chapter that although participants widely reported support needs and a desire to change how they behaved in relationships, few would have been at the threshold for a perpetrator intervention. This leads us to argue for a more holistic, 'relationships services' approach to responding to different types of IPVA. We discuss participants' help-seeking experiences and barriers, including those related to the intersections between being LGB and/or T+ and other aspects of their identities and biographies. Finally, we introduce the Coral Project Power, Control and Space for Reaction Wheel as a new tool for practitioners. Accompanying this are recommendations for providing more nuanced, safer and inclusive responses to LGB and/or T+ people who are experiencing and/or enact-

© The Author(s) 2020
C. Donovan, R. Barnes, *Queering Narratives of Domestic Violence and Abuse*, Palgrave
Studies in Victims and Victimology, https://doi.org/10.1007/978-3-030-35403-9_5

ing 'abusive' behaviours, many of which would enhance responses to heterosexual, cisgender people too.

Keywords Barriers to help-seeking • Coercive control • Counselling and psychotherapy • Couples counselling • Domestic violence and abuse • Domestic violence perpetrator programmes • Ecological approach • Intersectionality • Intimate partner violence and abuse • Lesbian, gay, bisexual and/or transgender • LGBT-inclusive services • Power and control wheel • Space for reaction • Typologies of domestic violence and abuse • Victims/survivors

5.1   Introduction

In this chapter we unpack the implications of our findings for policy and practice. Although we begin by outlining current policy and practice regarding LGB and/or T+ intimate partner violence and abuse (IPVA) and also perpetrators of domestic violence and abuse (DVA) within the UK, particularly England and Wales (see Barnes and Donovan 2016 for a fuller account), we ultimately argue that responding to the different types of IPVA that we have identified in this book requires involvement from a wider range of what we refer to as 'relationships services'. Many of our LGB and/or T+ participants would not meet the threshold for a specialist DVA service, perpetrator intervention or crisis responses such as police involvement or refuge provision, yet they nonetheless identify support needs which cannot currently be readily met. As we will show, the most frequently used formal support was counselling and psychotherapy, but we argue that this potentially individualises relationship troubles and may lack sufficient expertise to assess how violence, abuse, power and control operate in intimate relationships. We offer a new practitioner resource—the Coral Project Power, Control and Space for Reaction Wheel—and we make recommendations for providing more nuanced, safer and inclusive responses to LGB and/or T+ people who are experiencing and/or enacting 'abusive' behaviours, many of which would be beneficial for heterosexual cisgender (HC) people too.

5.2 The Current Policy and Practice Context for Responding to LGB and/or T+ DVA

In England and Wales, 'same-sex' couples were included in the landmark *Domestic Violence, Crime and Victims Act 2004*, which made civil remedies available to all victims, regardless of gender or sexuality, or of whether or not they were married, civilly partnered, or cohabiting. Subsequent legislation such as the recent *Serious Crime Act 2015*, which criminalised coercive and controlling behaviour in an intimate relationship, is also gender- and sexuality-neutral, as is the statutory definition of DVA being proposed in the draft *Domestic Abuse Bill 2019* (Home Office 2019a). This, in parallel with the progression of equality legislation (see Chap. 1), an increasing evidence base about LGB and/or T+ victim/survivors' experiences, and awareness-raising and training from LGBT+ and some DVA agencies, has led to mainstream services improving their awareness of and ability to respond appropriately to LGB and/or T+ victims/survivors. Less common is bespoke LGB and/or T+ provision, such as specialist independent domestic violence advisers and the national Galop helpline. However, the rigid victim/perpetrator binary that we have critiqued means that many of these specialist DVA services will not work with people who are, or who may be assessed as being, perpetrators.

Importantly, there are contradictions between a legislative context which is, at least on paper, LGBT+ inclusive and a policy context that has, certainly in England (Home Office 2009, 2016), Wales (Welsh Government 2016) and Scotland (Scottish Government and COSLA 2009, 2018), adopted a largely HC gendered approach. The Home Office (2009, 2016) policies fleetingly recognise the multiple disadvantages that LBT+ women who experience DVA may face but do not recognise GBT+ men (though see Home Office 2019b, which provides a more thorough analysis of GBT+ male victims' needs, beyond what has been set out so far for LBT+ women). The Northern Irish DVA policy contrastingly adopts a gender-neutral and sexuality-inclusive approach, recognising particular risks to LGB victims (DHSSPS and DoJ 2016). It follows that, in most parts of the UK, the limited discussion of perpetrators that has occurred has implicitly or explicitly focussed on HC perpetrators.

Moreover, responses to perpetrators over-rely on criminal justice mechanisms, and the latest Home Office (2016) strategy gives mixed messages, on the one hand calling for 'appropriate perpetrator programmes, prison and probation rehabilitation approaches, and mental health interventions' (Home Office 2016, p. 23) to hold perpetrators accountable for their behaviour, but—citing concerns about the effectiveness of domestic violence perpetrator programmes (DVPPs)—inferring that local decisions need to be made about delivery of these services.

Due to a lack of coherent policy and legislation regarding perpetrator provision, insufficient funding and mixed views about DVPPs (Kelly and Westmarland 2015), the UK unsurprisingly lags behind North America when it comes to perpetrator provision, not only for LGB and/or T+ perpetrators and HC women, who are particularly underserved, but also for HC men. Accredited court-mandated DVPPs have only been available for (HC) men across all probation areas in England and Wales since 2006 (Home Office 2009), whilst the provision of programmes for HC men outside the criminal justice system was first noted in government policy in 2009, when it was reported that the national umbrella organisation for perpetrator programmes, Respect (founded in 2000), had accredited two programmes and established its telephone helpline for HC men seeking help with their violent behaviour (Home Office 2009). The landscape has improved, but it remains a postcode lottery, having been profoundly affected by sweeping austerity cuts since 2010 (see Clayton et al. 2015) and a parallel agenda to privatise offender rehabilitation (Gilbert 2013; Roberts 2018) and embed competitive tendering into third sector funding and service delivery (Donovan and Durey 2018). As early as 2012, Respect reported that 78% of projects providing DVPPs had to reduce how many perpetrators they could support (Towers and Walby 2012).

Regarding LGBT+-inclusive provision, our own online search for voluntary perpetrator interventions, conducted in 2012–2013, found 50 community-based services across the UK, although very few of these explicitly recognised LGB and/or T+ male or female perpetrators as potential service users,[1] and none advertised bespoke interventions for

---

[1] The Respect helpline is a national service for heterosexual and LGB men and women (http://respectphoneline.org.uk).

LGB and/or T+ perpetrators. In contrast, examples of bespoke provision for LGB and/or T+ perpetrators exist in North America: Mendoza and Dolan-Soto (2011) talk about the first 'same-sex batterers' programme being set up in New York in 1991 and a 'Partner Assault Response' programme being set up in Toronto in 2001. Within the criminal justice system in England and Wales there are still no accredited mandatory programmes for HC female or LGB and/or T+ perpetrators. Practitioners who deliver mandatory or voluntary DVA perpetrator programmes whom we interviewed in England, Wales and Scotland recounted isolated examples of one-to-one work with LGBT perpetrators, while one probation service had amended their accredited individual programme for perpetrators to address the particular needs of LGB and/or T perpetrators (see Cannon 2019 for an outline of similar ad hoc work in North America). However, most practitioners articulated that LGB and/or T+ perpetrators are currently underserved (Barnes and Donovan 2016; Donovan and Barnes 2019).

This current gap in provision leaves most LGB and/or T+ perpetrators at all levels of risk and need without access to an intervention which targets their abusive behaviour—thus failing to hold them accountable and reduce the risk that they pose to current and future partners and any children involved. Crucially though, it is not only these perpetrators who require support and/or intervention, as we next consider.

5.3   Participants' Support Needs

The Coral Project survey collected unique data on LGB and/or T+ people's reporting of 'problems' with their behaviour and an indicator of their 'readiness to change'. This data reveals an ostensibly very reflective sample. Across the sample, respondents widely reported that either they or somebody else had identified that they had a problem with anger, jealousy, trust and/or needing to be in control, with between 9.0% and 25.8% self-identifying with each of these different problems (see Table 5.1), indicating that many individuals may need support regarding their relationships.

Table 5.1 Comparison between self-identified and other-identified problems among the whole sample and high perpetration and high victimisation subgroups

Problem	Whole sample (n = 777–779)[a]		High perpetration (n = 40)		High victimisation (n = 37–39)	
	Self-identified (%)	Identified by 1+ other party[b] (%)	Self-identified (%)	Identified by 1+ other party (%)	Self-identified (%)	Identified by 1+ other party (%)
Anger	14.9	18.7	35.0	55.0	10.3	17.9
Jealousy	9.0	11.5	12.5	30.0	5.1	12.8
Trusting others	25.8	25.2	37.5	52.5	30.8	28.2
Needing to be in control	13.8	15.7	35.0	47.5	12.8	7.7

[a]Valid n varied slightly for each problem
[b]Other parties included friends, current partner, previous partner, family or someone else

Identification of problems was substantially higher among the high perpetration subgroup: approximately half reported that one or more parties had identified that they had a problem with anger (55.0%) or needing to be in control (47.5%), whilst 35.0% self-identified each of these problems. Trusting others was the most frequently reported problem among the high victimisation group (self-identified by 30.8% of respondents); this is unsurprising, since especially for those who had experienced coercively controlling violence (CCV), loss of trust is a common experience (Herman 2015) (see Table 5.1). These findings usefully highlight the greater need for interventions to target individuals' need to be in control among those who are using violence and/or 'abusive' behaviours more extensively. Simultaneously though, such findings reinforce our message that 'perpetrators' are heterogeneous and that not everyone who enacts violence and 'abusive' behaviours struggles with needing to be in control; hence, a nuanced assessment of needs is essential.

A note of caution is required, however. If the 'problem' has been identified by an (ex-)partner, it cannot be ruled out that telling a partner that they are too angry or mistrusting, for example, is part of the belittling or accusatory tactics of a coercively controlling partner. It is also important to understand what it means for an individual to be struggling with one or more of these 'problems'. For example, rather than immediately recommending that someone who reports struggling with anger should attend anger management therapy, it is important to first explore how and why they experience anger. As discussed in Chap. 4, Clare reported feeling increasingly angry in response to her ex-partner's CCV towards her. However, given our categorisation of her behaviour as violent and non-violent resistance which sought to create space for reaction in response to a coercively controlling partner, it would not meet her needs—and could accentuate her self-blame—to refer her to anger management. Despite these caveats, what this data firmly shows is the common identification—by self and others—of struggles with intimate relationships which may or may not need external support, but for which, as we will later argue, appropriate and inclusive support is typically lacking.

The survey also used a 'readiness to change' indicator (modified from Rollnick et al. 1992) that posed six statements to elicit respondents' perceptions of whether they felt the need to change their behaviour, and whether they had already taken steps to do so. Substantial proportions of the whole sample endorsed readiness to change statements. Those in the high perpetration subgroup were most likely to problematise their behaviour, showing highest disagreement (19.4%) with the statement 'I think my behaviour is acceptable', compared to 8.7% of the overall sample and 4.3% of the high victimisation subgroup. However, both the high victimisation and high perpetration subgroups were more likely than the overall sample to agree that they were taking action to change their behaviour, and both were much more likely to endorse the need for change. For example, only 14.9% of the overall sample strongly agreed/agreed that 'I am at the stage where I should think about changing my behaviour', compared to 28.6% of the high victimisation and 32.3% of the high perpetration subgroups.

Data from the readiness to change statements was combined to produce a readiness to change score ranging from 6 (zero readiness to change) to 30 (the maximum readiness to change). Across the sample, scores ranged from 6 to 29, with a mean of 16.53 (standard deviation [SD] = 5.07). Readiness to change scores were highest for the high perpetration subgroup (mean = 19.81, SD = 4.35) than for the low perpetration (mean = 17.38, SD = 4.63) and no perpetration (mean = 12.92, SD = 4.6) subgroups, indicating a linear relationship between how those in the high perpetration group are more likely to recognise that their behaviour is problematic and either have taken or want to take steps to change their behaviour.

Importantly, this data captures respondents' perceptions of their need to change: whether or not they actually need to is not the central issue. For some, endorsement of these statements may stem from internalising victim-blaming messages and responsibilising themselves for perceived relationship failures. What we are interested in is the levels of demand among LGB and/or T+ people for relationships support and guidance, and how and where these demands are currently met (or unmet). Whilst this data shows a heightened recognition of the need for behaviour change in relationships, particularly among those who have most intensively experienced or used violence and 'abusive' behaviours, it also demonstrates that across the sample there is a considerable degree of self-reflection and recognition of the need to approach relationships differently. Thus, there is substantial demand for support for LGB and/or T+ people who want to change how they behave in, and/or improve the quality of, their intimate relationships. This raises the question of where they might receive appropriate and well-informed support to do so. We look more closely at this next when we consider participants' help-seeking experiences.

5.4   Help-Seeking Behaviour

Survey data was collected regarding help-seeking behaviours and barriers in relation to victimisation and perpetration; however, we focus on our novel data about the latter (see Donovan and Barnes in press; Donovan and Hester 2011, 2014; Guadalupe-Diaz and Jasinski 2017; Simpson and Helfrich 2014 for help-seeking for victimisation).

Respondents who indicated that they had used at least one 'abusive' behaviour ever were asked whether they had sought help and if so, from where. Free-text data on how helpful they found it was also collected. Overall, 41.3% of the 155 respondents who answered this question had sought help in relation to their use of 'abusive' behaviours. Corresponding to their elevated readiness to change scores (Sect. 5.3), 69.6% of the high perpetration subgroup had sought help in relation to their use of 'abusive' behaviours, compared to 33.9% of the low perpetration group. This emphasises the heterogeneity of 'perpetrators' and perpetration that we unpacked in Chaps. 3 and 4. Women were more likely to have sought help in relation to the behaviours that they had used (48.6%) compared to 37.0% of men, while the figure was considerably lower for trans+ respondents (30.8%). With regard to age, 16–24-year-olds were least likely to seek help in relation to their perpetration (31.4%). Thus, young people and trans+ people appear to be at the greatest risk of not receiving help to meet their needs.

Considering where help is sought, we focus only on recent help-seeking (within five years of completing the questionnaire). The most widely sought sources of support are friends and, to a lesser extent, family, and either National Health Service (NHS), private or third sector mental health services such as counselling and psychotherapy (see Table 5.2). Far

Table 5.2 Sources of help in relation to respondents' use of violence and 'abusive' behaviours

Sources of help used within the last five years	Frequency ($n = 64$)	%
Friends	38	59.4
NHS mental health	31	48.4
Private/third sector mental health	26	40.6
Family	25	39.1
Internet/web support	16	25.0
Health services	14	21.9
LGBT support service	11	17.2
Anger management	11	17.2
Someone at work	8	12.5
Other support[a]	7	10.9
The Samaritans	6	9.4
Women's DVA service	4	6.3
LGBT DVA service	2	3.1
Neighbours	1	1.6
Respect helpline	0	0.0
Men's DVA service	0	0.0

[a]Included a parenting helpline, a shamanic therapy course, sex and/or relationships therapists ($n = 3$) and meditation

fewer respondents reported seeking help from specialist LGBT and/or DVA services and none reported using the Respect domestic violence perpetrator helpline, although one interview participant reported having called it.

This emphasis on more 'individualised' or 'privatised' (see Donovan and Hester 2014, p. 174) sources of support echoes findings from the COHSAR research where, for victims/survivors of DVA, friends and counselling/therapy were the most frequently sought sources of support. Donovan and Hester drew comparisons with the Crime Survey for England and Wales (CSEW) data which indicate that (ostensibly HC) women are much more likely to seek support from family and public sector services (Donovan and Hester 2011, 2014). They argued that this stems from the legacy of the criminalisation and pathologisation of LGB lives, leaving LGB people reluctant to approach mainstream services due to a 'gap of trust'. Consequently, they argue that self-reliance has been a long-standing default position for LGB people (see Guadalupe-Diaz and Jasinski 2017 in relation to trans people), as is reinforced by our findings.

Fifty-five survey respondents offered free-text responses regarding which source of support they had found most helpful, and why. Individual and relationship counselling/psychotherapy was most often highlighted for helping respondents to work through difficulties, gain insight into their behaviours and develop relationship skills. For example:

> Most helpful has been counselling and learning how to communicate better (with my current partner—I now have a much better way of being with her).

> I found counselling helpful because it was private, confidential, impartial, non-judgemental, gently or directly challenging, helped me to explore/discover who I was, strengths & weaknesses, in certain aspects. I'd consider having more counselling in the future.

The benefits of gaining insight through counselling/psychotherapy were discussed at greater length in some of the interviews. The account of Adam, a white cisgender gay man in his mid-30s, was a complex one. Whilst we categorised him as a perpetrator of CCV (without any physical violence), this classification again highlights the limitations of the victim/

perpetrator binary. On the one hand, Adam detailed the 'cruel' and 'damaging' ways in which he would manipulate, sulk and belittle to get his own way in relationships. However, he also talked about being very sexually submissive, self-sacrificial and dissatisfied, and he recalled two relationships where he was forced into unwanted sex, and another where he was subjected to controlling and manipulative behaviour.

Adam attributed his ability to now talk with insight about his behaviour—including its adverse impacts on his former partners—to having long-term psychotherapy:

> [...] it's taken a therapist four years for me to actually start to unpick these things and I think if I hadn't have done that I'd probably still be in the same [passive-aggressive] patterns. Um and it still comes up, you know, I catch myself doing it, afterwards thinking 'Oh dammit I've done it again' so it is definitely still a behaviour I do.

Conversely, his experiences of victimisation occurred in relationships where he had strong feelings for his partners and felt desperate to please them. Adam reported other lifestyle changes—giving up alcohol and Grindr (a hook-up app for men who have sex with men) in his attempt to achieve his desire for 'power-sharing' relationships.

For other survey respondents, friends, and sometimes family, were also widely mentioned as being most helpful, partly because of having a close knowledge of the respondent and insights which come from observation of their relationship(s). Talking to people who had shared similar experiences was noted by some respondents as being especially valuable. However, the sources that were the most helpful for some respondents were identified by others as being the least helpful. Some respondents stated that friends and family had not been helpful because they did not have enough of an understanding of what was happening in the relationship to advise helpfully, or because of feeling judged or not listened to. Counselling and mental health services were most often criticised because of issues of accessibility, inappropriate referrals and long waiting lists, while one trans respondent wrote that their counsellor had been transphobic.

Very few participants had sought support from a specialist DVA service, although it is important to remember that the research is based on a convenience sample; hence, many respondents' experiences would fall below the threshold for a specialist DVA victim/survivor or perpetrator intervention. That said, 20 of the 36 interview participants gave accounts of being subjected to CCV, with three of these cases including police involvement and one participant granted a restraining order, yet even then, engagement with specialist DVA services was rare. This raises questions about how accessible and inclusive these services are—and appear to be—to LGB and/or T+ people, as well as how well-equipped they are to respond appropriately to LGB and/or T+ people's identities and intimate lives.

5.5   Unmet Needs and Participants' Views on Gaps in Support Provision

Survey respondents who reported that they had not sought help were asked about barriers to help-seeking. Table 5.3 shows what proportion of all of those who selected each reason for not seeking help identified as men, women or trans+, respectively. Reflecting trans+ respondents' lower rates of help-seeking, trans+ respondents were much more likely than cisgender women and men to identify multiple barriers. Trans+ respondents account for around a fifth of the respondents who answered this question, yet they were vastly over-represented in selecting 'Didn't think they could help' (42.9%) and 'Didn't think they would understand' (40.0%) (see Table 5.3). The disproportionate reporting of barriers points to particular challenges faced by those who are seen to deviate from the heteronormative, cisnormative heterosexual male/female binary. Moreover, we speculate that trans+ people's help-seeking decisions in relation to perpetration are likely to be constrained by concerns about fuelling negative stereotypes of trans people, particularly trans women, at a time of heightened stigma and hatred towards trans people (see Chap. 1).

Interview participants commonly expressed concerns about the capacity of help providers to understand their lives and identities. For example, Amber shared her lack of confidence that mainstream counsellors/thera-

Table 5.3 Barriers to help-seeking for perpetration by gender identity

Reason for not seeking help[a]	Men (n = 31)		Women (n = 31)		Trans+ (n = 17)		Total number of respondents[b]	
	Frequency	%[c]	Frequency	%	Frequency	%	Frequency	%
It wasn't serious enough to seek help	20	42.6	17	36.2	10	21.3	47	100.0
Private matter/nobody else's business	9	36.0	10	40.0	6	24.0	25	100.0
Didn't think they could help	5	23.8	7	33.3	9	42.9	21	100.0
Felt too ashamed	7	33.3	6	28.6	8	38.1	21	100.0
Didn't think they would understand	5	25.0	7	35.0	8	40.0	20	100.0
Didn't know where to go	8	50.0	3	18.8	5	31.3	16	100.0
Because of my sexuality	5	50.0	2	20.0	3	30.0	10	100.0
Because of my gender identity	1	20.0	0	0.0	4	80.0	5	100.0

[a]Some items are not shown due to very small numbers, for example, concerns about confidentiality and previous bad response from an agency

[b]Respondents could select multiple reasons, hence the frequencies exceed the valid n

[c]The total number of respondents selecting each of these reasons is in many cases very small, hence these percentages should be cited with great caution

pists would understand dynamics that are relevant to some lesbian relationships, explaining that she would therefore favour a specialist LGBT+ service because:

> It would have more of an insight into the things that we are facing [pause] like you talked about that butch-femme dynamic, I don't see many mainstream therapists having much of an understanding of that. (Amber, mixed ethnicity, cisgender lesbian, early 40s)

For Beth and Judy, their concerns related to their experiences of polyamorous (poly) and bondage, discipline, sadism and masochism (BDSM) relationships. Judy, a white, cisgender bisexual woman in her mid-20s, recalled that a specialist sexual violence service that predominantly served HC women had told her that so long as she continued to have BDSM relationships, she would keep being abused, which she found retraumatising and disempowering. Further, Beth explained that being in a poly, BDSM relationship had shut down options for seeking support:

> I wouldn't really know who to go to, it's difficult enough to be taken seriously with depression anyway, I mean when you try and throw in the fact you're in a BDSM relationship or a poly relationship they sort of look at you like you've grown another head sort of thing. (Beth, white, bisexual trans woman, early 30s)

In addition to fearing stigma because of her relationship type, Beth comments that having mental health needs makes it harder to receive suitable help. This highlights the importance of understanding help-seeking intersectionally by recognising the different and interrelating social positions (Crenshaw 1991; Fish 2008) that LGB and/or T+ people occupy. The complexity of negotiating multiple aspects of identity was a strong feature of Patricia's account which was discussed in Chap. 4. Her account powerfully communicates the deep mistrust of services, concerns about confidentiality and lack of appropriate avenues for seeking help:

> [B]ut in terms of support there's no one. Um would I go to a therapist? No. Would I go to a white therapist? You've got to be joking. Would I go to a black therapist to have all my business chucked around the community? No. Would I go to a straight woman? No. Would I go to Samaritans? I

think I phoned Samaritans once and the voice was so middle class—it's terrible I shouldn't do this but it was so distant from who I am—I just couldn't even say anything to them…there isn't—I would, I think if I could go to the Church and maybe do a confession where I'm just talking and no one says anything. (Patricia, mixed ethnicity, cisgender lesbian, late 40s)

Whilst participants more commonly reported concerns about being misunderstood on a personal level, some participants expressed a reluctance to 'air their dirty laundry in public' as an LGB and/or T+ person, because of concerns about giving the LGBT+ 'community' a bad name if domestic abuse or other relationship difficulties became known. Clare, whose relationship we discussed at some length in Chap. 4 explains:

I think there's, there's a, a reluctance actually for a lot of gay people to admit that there are problems, because you don't want to give gay relationships (short laugh) a bad press, you know. (Clare, white, bisexual cisgender woman, mid 30s)

This fear of damaging the reputation of LGB and/or T+ people and their relationships and potentially fuelling homo/bi/transphobia has been a recurring theme in the LGB and/or T+ DVA literature, and reinforces the reality that the social acceptance of LGB and/or T+ people and their relationships remains contingent and insecure, thus leading to the silencing of relationship difficulties (Duke and Davidson 2009; Hart 1986; Ristock 2002). On a similar theme of community loyalties, Angela explained that she and her partner felt pressure from their lesbian peers not to split up because they were role models for having a long-lasting and ostensibly successful same-sex relationship.

In another case, Eddie, a white, cisgender bisexual man in his late 20s, explained that he and his then partner were thwarted by a postcode lottery when they tried to access relationship support from their nearest voluntary LGBT agency, because that agency was not funded to provide services to people in their area. This instance reflects the impact on voluntary services—and, disproportionately, on those services serving minority populations such as LGB and/or T+ people—of austerity-driven commissioning agendas that leave people falling between the cracks and with unmet needs (Colgan et al. 2014; Mitchell et al. 2013).

Notably, whilst our categorisation of interview participants' accounts suggests that the vast majority of participants are not at the threshold for, and would not benefit from, a perpetrator intervention, we categorised two participants as having given accounts of perpetrating CCV. In addition to Adam, discussed above, the other was Brenda, a white, cisgender lesbian in her early 60s, who talked about having often felt criticised and disrespected by her partners, and having responded with anger. This had been most heightened in her 18-month relationship with her ex-partner, Pauline. Brenda described Pauline as controlling, but she described her own behaviour in that relationship as 'extraordinary' and she thought that they had both behaved 'abusively'. She described Pauline as setting the terms for the relationship regarding when they would see each other and what they would do. Pauline would reportedly use Brenda for practical and emotional support due to her poor health but would not then want to spend time socially with her, leaving Brenda feeling rejected and used. Yet, Brenda talks about not being interested in getting to know Pauline's family or her friends: she wanted Pauline to want to spend all her time with her, as Brenda did with Pauline. Brenda's abusive behaviour also included throwing car keys at Pauline in the supermarket, driving aggressively in a way that frightened Pauline, and on one occasion frightening Pauline by refusing to leave her house when Pauline asked her to during an argument. In the survey, Brenda was in the high perpetration subgroup.

Brenda and Pauline engaged in couples counselling; but Brenda also contacted a DVA organisation for perpetrators who told her that she was a perpetrator and that she should attend a perpetrator programme. Whilst she reported feeling 'a bit stunned' by the suggestion that she might be a perpetrator, she had been open to attending and exploring the dynamics of her relationship. However, the nearest programme for women was over 70 miles away, reflecting the postcode lottery for perpetrator provision more generally, but the especially limited provision for both HC women and LGB and/or T+ people. She had received some one-to-one counselling by the time of the interview, but was concerned that she would behave similarly in her new relationship. This is a clear example of unmet need with regard to someone who has a history of behaving in very controlling, verbally aggressive and intimidating ways in her relationships, and is concerned about continuing to do so.

5.6 Involving a Wider Range of Relationships Services in Preventing and Responding to LGB and/or T+ People's Experiences of IPVA

Existing policy and practice primarily focusses on CCV, or DVA, as the most extreme form of IPVA (see Sect. 5.2), and yet this overlooks the needs of those LGB and/or T+ people who are experiencing and/or enacting other types of IPVA. Most survey respondents who reported using violence or 'abusive' behaviours did so relatively infrequently, and unlike many HC male perpetrators of DVA towards HC women (e.g. Kelly and Westmarland 2015), most favoured equality in decision-making in their intimate relationships (see Chap. 3). However, as demonstrated above, participants acknowledged clear support needs but were typically not aware of where they could receive suitable support.

Telling different stories about IPVA means that we need to consider what the overarching narratives are about help-seeking for IPVA. The feminist DVA literature rightly emphasises that it is dangerous for people in coercively controlling relationships to attend relationship counselling. This is partly due to the risk both of the counsellor/therapist being manipulated into colluding with the perpetrator, and of reinforcing victim-blaming messages by holding both parties responsible for relationship difficulties (see Tomsich et al. 2015; Trute 1998). Consequently, many relationship counselling and support organisations refuse to work with couples where CCV is ongoing. However, recognition that there are different types of IPVA, such as Johnson's (2008) category of situational couple violence (SCV), has prompted questions about whether relationship counselling may be appropriate for IPVA that is not CCV, subject to ongoing monitoring of risk (Tavistock Relationships 2016; Karakurt et al. 2016). However, not all providers of relationship and individual counselling/psychotherapy have been trained in such nuanced understandings of IPVA, risk assessment or safety planning, or consider this a part of their professional practice.

As noted above, seeking individual or relationship counselling/psychotherapy was the most common avenue for formal help-seeking. A focus on counselling and psychotherapy alone, however, arguably individual-ises the issues which LGB and/or T+ people are encountering in their relationships. As we have argued, relationship norms and expectations are socially constructed, and thus relationship problems and behaviours need to be understood through a sociological lens, and not purely a psycho-logical one. Moreover, free counselling is increasingly difficult to access, and a typical offer of six sessions is unlikely to be effective, whilst the cost of private counselling/psychotherapy is prohibitive for many people. Therefore, whilst one of our key recommendations is that counsellors and psychotherapists need to receive more specialist training on the dynamics of LGB and/or T+ people's relationships, different types of IPVA, risk assessment and safety planning, more multi-agency and holistic approaches need to complement the availability of counselling/psychotherapy.

Specifically, what we call for is greater multi-agency involvement from those who deliver what we call 'relationships services'—that is, any ser-vice which offers advice, education and support that is pertinent to peo-ple's intimate relationships and lives (Donovan et al. 2014; see also Relate 2016). Thus, as well as specialist DVA services and relationship and indi-vidual counselling/psychotherapy, this includes (not exhaustively) those delivering formal relationships and sex education (RSE) in schools as well as informal RSE delivered by youth workers and in further and higher education settings (see Universities UK 2016), HIV and sexual health services, substance misuse services, social services, housing services and family support services. This more holistic approach would enable people who are in relationships where there is IPVA to start to recognise their victimisation and/or the impacts of their own IPVA, and to receive appro-priate input and (where necessary) cross-referral or signposting to specialist DVA services or other agencies. Further, there is also a key role for these relationships services to play in preventative work to educate LGB and/or T+ people about intimate relationships, and to thus help them to be less vulnerable to aspects of the experiential power which we discussed in Chap. 4, whereby an abusive partner can become the main or sole source of information about being in an intimate relationship as an LGB and/or T+ person.

Within this, there are three key areas where we make recommendations to maximise the quality, safety and appropriateness of the responses that are provided.

5.6.1 Recognising and Responding to Different Types of Violence and Abuse

A consistent thread in this book has been the emphasis on the heterogeneity of IPVA. A growing literature highlights the difficulties which practitioners face in assessing IPVA and understanding how power and control operate in intimate relationships. Risk assessment practices, most often conducted by the police, typically reflect incident-based understandings of DVA and therefore risk overlooking the 'golden thread' of coercive control (Myhill and Kohl 2016; see also Robinson et al. 2018). However, since coercive and controlling behaviour in intimate relationships was criminalised across the UK, questions have been raised about how well-equipped frontline practitioners are to detect coercive control (Barlow et al. 2019; Brennan et al. 2019; Robinson et al. 2018). These shortcomings reveal urgent training needs, since failure to recognise coercive control can lead to victim/survivors' experiences of chronic, highly pernicious violence and abuse to be minimised and invisibilised. In the most extreme cases, failure to recognise coercive control has been related to missed warning signs in situations that culminate in domestic homicide (Johnson et al. 2019; Sharp-Jeffs and Kelly 2016; Stark 2007).

Challenges in detecting coercive control not only apply to HC people's relationships; practitioners' assessments of IPVA within LGB and/or T+ people's intimate relationships can be shaped by incorrect assumptions that the violence and abuse are not as serious and less likely to escalate (see Chap. 1). Other misperceptions of LGB and/or T+ people's relationships, such as the assumption of mutual abuse, are considered shortly. It is particularly important that practitioners avoid either consciously or subconsciously determining who 'the victim' and 'the perpetrator' are on the basis of a superficial presentation of gender as embodied in the public story of DVA (Donovan and Hester 2014). Further, practitioners need to be mindful that LGB and/or T+ victims/survivors may not recognise their own victimisation because of the dominance in the public story of DVA of the HC female/male and victim/perpetrator binaries as discussed in Chap. 4.

Because of concerns about mis-identifying victims/survivors and perpetrators, specialist assessment tools have been developed for use by and for practitioners who are working with LGB and/or T+ people (see Hodes and Mennicke 2019). One such tool is Donovan and Hester's COHSAR Power and Control (P&C) Wheel (Donovan and Hester 2014, p. 205). The COHSAR P&C Wheel is based on the original Duluth P&C Wheel (see Domestic Abuse Intervention Project 2017). The original Duluth P&C Wheel was developed by the Domestic Abuse Intervention Project in Duluth, Minnesota (Pence and Shephard 1999). The wheel both emphasises the relationship between (HC) men's abuse of women and (HC) women's unequal position of power in wider society and challenges an incident-based focus which reifies physical violence and invisibilises the overarching power and control dynamics of the relationship. It has been used extensively with both HC female victims/survivors, and with HC male perpetrators of DVA, to increase understanding of abusive relationship dynamics (Pence and Shephard 1999). More broadly, it demonstrates an ecological approach which combines individual, relationship and social-structural factors (Heise 1998).

Multiple versions of this wheel have subsequently been developed (see Donovan and Hester 2014) to tailor it to the needs of different groups of victims/survivors of DVA including a LGBT P&C Wheel (Roe and Jadoginsky, n.d.) which takes into account identity abuse related to sexuality and gender identity and adds an additional layer of homo/bi/transphobia and heterosexism to the wheel to illustrate how DVA is compounded by these structural violences. The COHSAR P&C Wheel (Donovan and Hester 2014, p. 205) features:

- The two relationship rules at the centre of the wheel (see Fig. 5.1), as the core assumptions that underpin a DVA relationship;
- A hub of power and control which surrounds the relationship rules and signals that it is through this that the rules are maintained;
- Eleven spokes which capture the behaviours that may be used by a perpetrator of DVA to maintain their coercive control (mirrored in

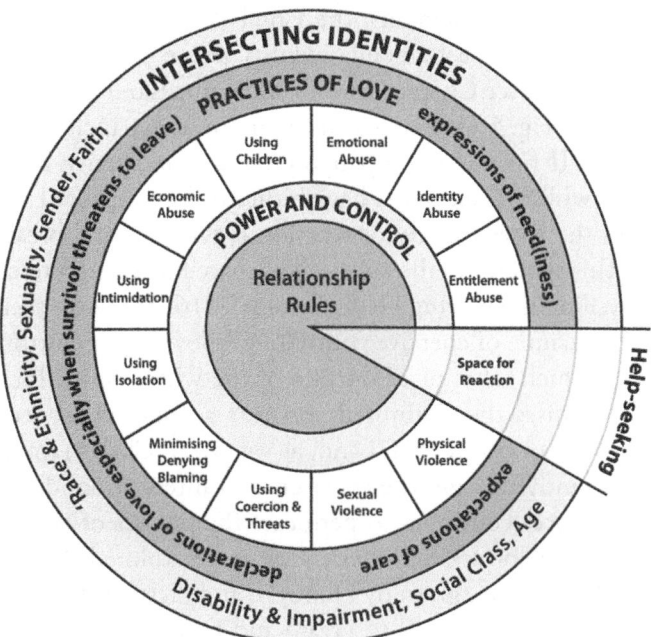

Fig. 5.1 The Coral Project Power, Control and Space for Reaction Wheel (adapted from the COHSAR Power and Control Wheel, originally published in Catherine Donovan and Marianne Hester, *Domestic Violence and Sexuality: What's Love Got to Do with It?* (p. 205). Republished with permission of Policy Press (an imprint of Bristol University Press, UK)

Fig. 5.1). The spoke of 'male privilege' in the original Duluth P&C Wheel was split into identity abuse and entitlement abuse.

- A layer of practices of love which surround these eleven spokes (as in Fig. 5.1) and includes such interventions as declarations of love and expressions of neediness made by the abusive partner, which enable them to neutralise, normalise or distract from their abusive and controlling behaviour;
- A final outer layer of intersecting identities, as mirrored in Fig. 5.1, which moves beyond Roe and Jadoginsky's (n.d.) inclusion only of homo/bi/transphobia and heterosexism but recognises the more complex social positions resulting from individuals' multiple and intersecting identities.

In addition to these elements, the Coral Project Power, Control and Space for Reaction Wheel amends identity abuse to include the use of experiential power (see Chaps. 1 and 4) and embeds our concept of space for reaction (see Fig. 5.1) as well as using more trans+-inclusive language (see Appendix II for the accompanying table of indicative behaviours). Importantly, whilst all elements have hitherto been captured within the perimeter of the wheel, space for reaction is different and breaks out of the wheel. This symbolises the *potential* of space for reaction to take steps towards 'levelling the playing field' (Velonis 2016, p. 1046), thereby disrupting the dynamic of coercive control and providing opportunities for help-seeking which takes place outside of the wheel. Space for reaction therefore recognises the victimised partner's agency, whilst recognising also that it may not be successful and, as we saw in Chap. 4, may be very costly. Importantly though, the experience of intersecting identities and structural violences continues to permeate the process of creating space for reaction and help-seeking experiences, as we explored above.

Echoing the guidance given by Donovan and Hester (2014), the Coral Project wheel is not intended to create and fix an 'ideal type' for what constitutes a relationship characterised by CCV. Rather, it is intended to be more indicative of the different behaviours and practices that perpetrators of CCV may draw on—and to recognise how what might appear to be the victimised partner's use of 'abusive' behaviours may actually be their creation of space for reaction in a coercively controlling relationship. Thus, recognising that the relationship rules, practices of love and their enactment of violent and non-violent resistance as part of creating space for reaction may inhibit a victim/survivor of CCV from recognising their victimisation is critical. Using the Coral Project wheel can therefore help to conduct more nuanced assessments of how violence, 'abusive' behaviours and power and control are operating in a relationship context and to avoid mis-labelling someone who is being victimised, but who may not see themselves and their relationship in this way, as either a perpetrator or as someone who does not need any support.

Relatedly, the public story of DVA which produces overlaying binaries of HC male/female, perpetrator/victim mean that victims/survivors of DVA are often operating with very narrow definitions of victimhood and DVA. It is vital, therefore, that marketing, awareness-raising and training materials for DVA services make clear that being a victim does not mean that they are, or would inevitably feel, defenceless and blameless; and that the strength and resourcefulness of victims/survivors in creating space for reaction are highlighted. It is also important to strike a balance between privileging and respecting a service user or client's understanding of their relationship, while recognising that their perceptions may result, at least in part, from their partner's 'definitional hegemony' over the relationship (Lempert 1997). This point is grounded in a number of the accounts discussed in Chap. 4, for example, where Marcus and Clare often placed a strong emphasis on problematising their own behaviour and were subsequently reluctant to identify that they had been victimised by DVA.

Whilst our focus here is on reducing instances of LGB and/or T+ people being assumed to be in mutually abusive relationships when they are actually being victimised by CCV and need help to maximise their safety and recognise their victimisation, Hodes and Mennicke (2019) raise another crucial concern. This is that those who are experiencing what they call 'escalated conflict', which can be likened to Johnson's (2008) SCV, will be incorrectly labelled as victims or perpetrators and may subsequently be channelled into inappropriate interventions (e.g. perpetrator programmes) that may have negative impacts. However, this does not mean that partners in relationships where there is escalated conflict, or SCV, do not need support. In our own survey, a third of the low perpetration subgroup, which includes those whose experiences reflect SCV, had sought help for their own perpetration behaviour. Leone et al.'s (2014) study of 389 low-income HC women in Chicago found that 70.2% of victims of CCV had sought formal help compared to 44.4% of victims of SCV, and that victims of SCV were more likely to say that help was not needed. Further, victims of CCV were more likely to identify fear of further abuse as a barrier to seeking help, although 10.7% of victims of SCV (compared to 31.0% of victims of CCV) identified fear as a barrier to contacting the police. Hence, whilst there are dominant trends which locate fear more with CCV than SCV, it is important to be alert to a continuum of experience within each type of violence.

Leone et al. (2014) suggest that women experiencing SCV may not need any formal help and may instead be confident in handling the SCV or receiving advice from friends and family. We conversely argue that whilst those experiencing and/or enacting SCV may present as having fewer needs and posing less risk, this does not mean that they do not require a service; rather, it means that they do not *typically* require services which are targeted at victims/survivors of DVA who are deemed to be at greatest risk and in greatest need and/or who are in crisis situations. Similarly, Hodes and Mennicke (2019) stipulate that suitable interventions need to be available for couples experiencing escalated conflict, such as opportunities for 'healthy relationship skill-building', mediation and couples counselling that are geographically and financially accessible and inclusive of the needs of diverse communities. Therefore, the more holistic relationships services that we call for should include opportunities for formal support that bridges a crisis response and reliance on friends and family who may not be equipped to provide appropriate advice or signposting. One of Walby and Towers' (2018) critiques of Johnson's typology (see Chap. 1) is its treatment of different types of IPVA as static. Because this typology has only been applied cross-sectionally, rather than longitudinally, it is not possible to determine whether there is, for example, escalation from SCV to CCV, though Leone et al. (2014) do not discount this possibility; and Hodes and Mennicke (2019) argue that there is. Therefore, interventions for SCV may serve to prevent this escalation by equipping couples to manage conflict in a non-abusive, power-sharing way.

Early intervention is consequently vital, and this is reinforced by Relate, Relationships Scotland and Marriage Care's (2017) report on the state of relationships in the UK. Based on a poll of 5071 adults across the UK, a quarter of respondents were in what authors termed 'distressed' intimate relationships, which the authors argue have adverse physical and mental health implications, as well as negative impacts on the wellbeing and development of any children. However, 40% of respondents said that they would not know where to access relationships support, and only 22% were open to seeking professional support for relationship difficulties. Moreover, there is evidence of ongoing stigma attached to seeking relationships support, reflected in 54% of respondents saying that if they did seek professional relationships support, they would not want anybody to know about it. It is therefore unsurprising that Relate (2016) report that couples typically seek relationship counselling only when they are in a state of crisis, at which stage it may be too late to deal with entrenched patterns and issues. Therefore, a cultural change in how intimate relationships are understood is needed, with priorities being to embed inclusive RSE in schools; to normalise discussion of relationship difficulties in order to alleviate stigma; and to improve the availability, accessibility and appropriateness of relationships services, with nuanced and ongoing assessments of safety being central to this provision.

5.6.2   Providing LGBT+-Inclusive Services

The context of heteronormativity, cisnormativity and LGBT+ invisibility poses barriers to LGB and/or T+ people seeking help from agencies where they may fear hostile or unhelpful responses and/or where they may not be able to 'see themselves' in that service. As previously discussed, the public story of DVA (Donovan and Hester 2014) can be particularly inhibiting for LGB and/or T+ people when it comes to accessing specialist DVA services for either victims/survivors or perpetrators. More generally, LGB and/or T+ people may be deterred from accessing support if their relationships are not visible in an agency's written material or visual representations of who is catered for. Further, echoing Weeks et al.'s (2001) concept of 'community knowledges', being known to have LGB and/or T+ staff or partner relationships with specialist LGB and/or T+ agencies, is also important for instilling trust in potential LGB and/or T+ service users that a particular agency will understand their lives and not stigmatise them (see Donovan and Barnes in press).

As discussed earlier in this chapter, many participants such as Amber expressed a preference for specialist LGBT+ services, believing that specialist services would better understand LGBT+ identities and intimate lives. However, others felt that LGBT+ specialist services were ghettoising and that mainstream services ought to be able to meet their needs. It is, however, unfortunately very clear both from this and other research (see also Calton et al. 2016) that mainstream services are not visible or approachable to many LGB and/or T+ people, and that their needs are often not met.

In order to increase accessibility to LGB and/or T+ people, the outward presentation of an agency and its services needs to adopt language, imagery and symbols which communicate to LGB and/or T+ people that they are included (Duke and Davidson 2009) and that their intimate lives and support needs will be understood. Awareness-raising and out-reach efforts should not be restricted to LGB and/or T+ social spaces and resources, as this would stop these messages from reaching those who are marginalised from (Simpson and Helfrich 2014)—or indeed, in cases of CCV, isolated from—these spaces. However, this outwardly inclusive presentation needs to be consolidated by staff who are culturally compe-tent and affirming of LGB and/or T+ people. Good, comprehensive, face-to-face training is therefore essential. Duke and Davidson (2009) propose a useful framework for training advocates which does not only include content about the particularities of LGB and/or T+ people's experiences of DVA and actively names and challenges myths such as that of mutual abuse, but also considers barriers to help-seeking and how to create a safe environment for service delivery, as well as how to increase the accessibility of services. Avoiding using language which perpetuates the heterosexual cisnormative assumption is important (i.e. not assuming the gender identity or sexuality of the service user/client or their partner) as such assumptions can silence LGB and/or T+ people and reinforce fears about not being understood (Duke and Davidson 2009; Simpson and Helfrich 2014). In addition, specific needs which need to be addressed include ensuring that the LGB and/or T+ person's level of outness is fac-tored into their safety plan, where needed (Calton et al. 2016).

Key themes which arose from our interviews with practitioners involved in delivering perpetrator programmes primarily for HC men included whether LGB and/or T+ perpetrators were considered to need the same or different responses, or a mix of the two. The lack of established practice means that there are no precedents for working with LGB and/or T+ people who have used 'abusive' behaviours. Issues for practitioners included: whether entirely different course content would be required or whether existing materials for HC men could be adapted through using LGBT-inclusive language and examples; and whether LGB and/or T+ participants (and in particularly, male GB and/or T+ men) could be incorporated into existing groups or would need their own groups. We echo the safety concerns which several practitioners raised in relation to the risk of exposing GB and/or T men to homo/bi/transphobia if they were included in groups for HC men, while questioning how effective an intervention would be if GB and/or T participants felt unable to talk openly about their identities and lives in this setting. Yet, advocating for LGBT-specific groups raises further considerations of whether women and men should be in separate groups, and how best to include trans+ service users. These issues are rather abstract in the current context where practitioners reported very limited demand for these specialist services. However, if services do adopt these proposed recommendations and more LGB and/or T+ people come forward, ensuring the safety, accessibility and effectiveness of support and interventions for them, especially where group work is involved, will require careful consideration; as well as providing support for their victimised (ex)partners (Barnes and Donovan 2016; Donovan and Barnes 2019).

5.6.3 Supporting LGB and/or T+ People at the Intersections

As discussed throughout this book, an intersectional approach which recognises how people's sexualities and gender identities intersect with their multiple other identities such as their social class, 'race', faith, age, disability or citizenship status, along with other factors such as whether they are a parent, in their first same-sex, bisexual and/or transgender relationship, and their geographical location, is critical. Services need to be able to recognise both the intersecting dimensions of privilege and disadvantage which shape LGB and/or T+ people's experiences, and accordingly, differences not only *between* LGB and/or T+ people and HC people, but also *across* LGB and/or T+ people (Formby 2017). For example, whilst some LGB and/or T+ people may find that LGBT+ social and support spaces are places where they feel understood, for Black, Asian and minority ethnic LGB and/or T+ people they can be spaces where racism is rife; while for LGB and/or T+ people with disabilities, they can be physically inaccessible and discriminatory (Stonewall 2018).

Therefore, LGB and/or T+ people's social locations will either alleviate or exacerbate barriers to seeking formal or informal support. As discussed previously, our survey data shows that younger LGB and/or T+ people (16–24-year-olds) and trans+ people are least likely to seek help compared to older age groups and cisgender women and men, respectively. These findings about trans people's help-seeking are supported by other recent studies. Guadalupe-Diaz and Jasinski's (2017) study of the help-seeking experiences of 18 trans survivors in the USA found, in common with our own findings, that participants struggled to reconcile their identities with feminised constructions of victims who are weak, submissive and do not fight back. Whilst, as we have discussed, this can be an issue for other survivors too, it can take on particularly loaded meanings for trans survivors who are grappling with issues such as legitimacy and authenticity within their gender identities. Secondly, experiencing cisgenderist, transphobic discriminatory responses when using formal sources of help such as the police or courts was commonplace, while others were deterred from calling the police due to expectations of hostile responses, along with fears of not being believed or understood because of their trans identity and/or gender presentation. Further, because many specialist DVA services are organised around binary gender identities, trans+ people occupy a more tenuous position in terms of whether they will feel safe, accepted and understood within services designated as women-only or (less often) men-only (Calton et al. 2016; Guadalupe-Diaz and Jasinski 2017).

Additionally, our interview data highlighted how 'race' and ethnicity and geography restricted help-seeking options, whilst being in a BDSM and/or poly relationship also intensified a small number of participants' concerns about not being understood, or being pathologised. It is essential that practitioners and policymakers have an understanding of these, and other, intersectional barriers to help-seeking so that outreach to these groups can be effectively tailored, and so that holistic and inclusive responses can be provided.

5.7   Summary

This chapter has presented quantitative and qualitative data that enables us to argue the case that LGB and/or T+ people who are in relationships where there is IPVA are currently underserved and are unable to access support and interventions which meet their needs. Some of these arguments also resonate with issues facing HC people who are in relationships where there is IPVA: the lagging development and inconsistent availability of perpetrator programmes, even for HC male perpetrators of DV; the poor understanding of coercive control by practitioners such as the police; and the rationing of services to high-risk, extreme cases that have reached crisis point. These issues are accentuated for LGB and/or T+ people, because, as we have shown, studies of practitioners have found that, at least in 'same-sex' relationships, assumptions may be made that risk of harm and escalation is lower. However, the heteronormativity and cisnormativity of mainstream services that work with victims/survivors and, less often, perpetrators of DVA mean that LGB and/or T+ people can be deterred from seeking help due to concerns about their identities and relationships not being understood, as well as fears of being stigmatised or being disloyal by acknowledging relationship troubles as an LGB and/or T+ person.

As noted, the existing landscape for responding to IPVA is, in many respects understandably, focussed on using what limited resources are available—especially against the backdrop of ten years of austerity cuts—to respond to the highest risk cases of DVA. Consequently, there are few avenues, besides individual or relationship counselling/psychotherapy, for seeking formal help for other kinds of IPVA. Moreover, services that reflect the public story of DVA with rigid binaries of female/male, victim/perpetrator inhibit LGB and/or T+ people (and potentially also HC people) from seeking support in situations where they have been victimised but have also been able to create space for reaction, which may have involved their use of violent and 'abusive' behaviours in self-defence, retaliation or resistance.

The data that we have presented in this chapter provides compelling evidence that a substantial proportion of participants are motivated to take steps to change their behaviour in relationships: some are having detrimental relationship experiences, avoiding relationships or present a risk to current and future partners because they do not know where to go to receive appropriate, inclusive support. However, many of these individuals would not be at the threshold for receiving a DVA intervention. It is this tension which leads us to propose a model of 'relationships services' to provide a holistic, multi-agency response to relationship difficulties that can provide opportunities for improved, inclusive RSE and early intervention, before relationship conflicts and difficulties potentially escalate into abusive situations. Practitioners providing relationships services need to feel confident to assess whether and how violence, 'abusive' behaviours and power and control are operating in a relationship. It is here that the Coral Project Power, Control and Space for Reaction Wheel becomes a novel tool that we hope will enable practitioners to look beyond the reification of physical violence and a preoccupation with individual incidents rather than patterns of behaviour; understand how identity abuse and experiential power operate in LGB and/or T+ people's relationships, in conjunction with forms of oppression related to other intersecting identities; and assess whether what might be assumed to be a case of 'mutual abuse' is conversely a situation where a victimised partner is creating space for reaction.

We next move on to our conclusion, where the key messages of this book are synthesised, and future directions identified.

References

Barlow, C., Johnson, K., Walklate, S., & Humphreys, L. (2019, July 22). Putting coercive control into practice: Problems and possibilities. *The British Journal of Criminology*. https://doi.org/10.1093/bjc/azz041

Barnes, R., & Donovan, C. (2016). Developing interventions for abusive partners in lesbian, gay, bisexual and/or transgender relationships. In S. Hilder & V. Bettinson (Eds.), *Domestic violence: Interdisciplinary perspectives on protection, prevention and intervention* (pp. 297–320). Basingstoke: Palgrave Macmillan.

Brennan, I. R., Burton, V., Gormally, S., & O'Leary, N. (2019). Service provider difficulties in operationalizing coercive control. *Violence Against Women, 25*(6), 635–653.

Calton, J. M., Cattaneo, L. B., & Gebhard, K. T. (2016). Barriers to help seeking for lesbian, gay, bisexual, transgender, and queer survivors of intimate partner violence. *Trauma, Violence, and Abuse, 17*(5), 585–600.

Cannon, C. (2019). What services exist for LGBTQ perpetrators of intimate partner violence in batterer intervention programs across North America? A qualitative study. *Partner Abuse, 10*(2), 222–242.

Clayton, J., Donovan, C., & Merchant, J. (2015). Distancing and limited resourcefulness: Third sector service provision under austerity localism in the North East of England. *Urban Studies, 53*(4), 723–740.

Colgan, F., Hunter, C., & McKearney, A. (2014). *'Staying alive': The impact of 'austerity cuts' on the LGBT Voluntary and Community Sector (VCS) in England and Wales*. London: London Metropolitan University.

Crenshaw, K. (1991). Mapping the margins: Intersectionality, identity politics, and violence against women of color. *Stanford Law Review, 43*(6), 1241–1299.

Department of Health, Social Services and Public Safety and Department of Justice (DHSSPS and DoJ). (2016). *Stopping domestic and sexual violence and abuse in Northern Ireland: A seven year strategy*. Belfast: DHSSPS and DoJ.

Domestic Abuse Intervention Project. (2017). *Wheels*. Retrieved September 21, 2019, from https://www.theduluthmodel.org/wheels/

Donovan, C., & Barnes, R. (2019). Making sense of discourses of sameness and difference in agency responses to abusive LGB and/or T partners. *Sexualities, 22*(5–6), 785–802.

Donovan, C., & Barnes, R. (in press). Help-seeking among lesbian, gay, bisexual and/or transgender victims/survivors of domestic violence and abuse: The impacts of cisgendered heteronormativity and invisibility. *Journal of Sociology*. https://doi.org/10.1177/1440783319882088

Donovan, C., Barnes, R., & Nixon, C. (2014). *The Coral Project: Exploring abusive behaviours in lesbian, gay, bisexual and/or transgender relationships: Interim report*. Sunderland and Leicester: University of Sunderland and University of Leicester. Retrieved March 30, 2019, from https://www2.le.ac.uk/departments/criminology/documents/coral-project-interim-report

Donovan, C., & Durey, M. (2018). 'Well that would be nice, but we can't do that in the current climate': Prioritising services under austerity. In P. Rushton & C. Donovan (Eds.), *Austerity policies: Bad ideas in practice* (pp. 197–220). London: Palgrave Macmillan.

Donovan, C., & Hester, M. (2011). Seeking help from the enemy: Help-seeking strategies of those in same sex relationships who have experienced domestic abuse. *Child and Family Law Quarterly, 23*(1), 26–40.

Donovan, C., & Hester, M. (2014). *Domestic violence and sexuality: What's love got to do with it?* Bristol: Policy Press.

Duke, A., & Davidson, M. M. (2009). Same-sex intimate partner violence: Lesbian, gay and bisexual affirmative outreach and advocacy. *Journal of Aggression, Maltreatment and Trauma, 18*(8), 795–816.

Fish, J. (2008). Navigating queer street: Researching the intersections of Lesbian, Gay, Bisexual and Trans (LGBT) identities in health research. *Sociological*

Research Online, 13(1), 12. Retrieved August 17, 2019, from http://www.socresonline.org.uk/13/1/12.html

Formby, E. (2017). *Exploring LGBT spaces and communities: Contrasting identities, belongings and wellbeing.* Abingdon: Routledge.

Gilbert, B. (2013). Public protection? The implications of Grayling's 'Transforming Rehabilitation' agenda on the safety of women and children. *British Journal of Community Justice, 11*(2–3), 123–134.

Guadalupe-Diaz, X. L., & Jasinski, J. (2017). 'I wasn't a priority, I wasn't a victim': Challenges in help seeking for transgender survivors of intimate partner violence. *Violence Against Women, 23*(6), 772–792.

Hart, B. (1986). Lesbian battering: An examination. In K. Lobel (Ed.), *Naming the violence: Speaking out about lesbian battering* (pp. 173–189). Seattle: Seal Press.

Heise, L. (1998). Violence against women: An integrated, ecological framework. *Violence Against Women, 4,* 262–290.

Herman, J. (2015). *Trauma and recovery: The aftermath of violence—From domestic abuse to political terror.* New York, NY: Basic Books.

Hodes, C., & Mennicke, A. (2019). Is it conflict or abuse? A practice note for furthering differential assessment and response. *Journal of Clinical Social Work, 47*(2), 176–184.

Home Office. (2009). *Together we can end violence against women and girls: A strategy.* London: HMSO.

Home Office. (2016). *Ending violence against women and girls: Strategy 2016–2020.* Retrieved September 9, 2019, from https://assets.publishing.service.gov.uk/government/uploads/system/uploads/attachment_data/file/522166/VAWG_Strategy_FINAL_PUBLICATION_MASTER_vRB.PDF

Home Office. (2019a). *Transforming the response to domestic abuse: Consultation response and draft bill.* London: Crown Copyright. Retrieved September 27, 2019, from https://assets.publishing.service.gov.uk/government/uploads/system/uploads/attachment_data/file/772247/Transforming_the_response_to_domestic_abuse_-_consultation_response_and_draft_bill_-print.pdf

Home Office. (2019b). *Position statement on male victims of crimes considered in the cross-government strategy on ending violence against women and girls (VAWG).* Retrieved September 9, 2019, from https://assets.publishing.service.gov.uk/government/uploads/system/uploads/attachment_data/file/783996/Male_Victims_Position_Paper_Web_Accessible.pdf

Johnson, H., Eriksson, L., Mazerolle, P., & Wortley, R. (2019). Intimate femicide: The role of coercive control. *Feminist Criminology, 14*(1), 3–23.

Johnson, M. P. (2008). *A typology of domestic violence: Intimate terrorism, violent resistance, and situational couple violence.* Boston: Northeastern University Press.

Karakurt, G., Whiting, K., Van Esch, C., Bolen, S., & Calabrese, J. (2016). Couple therapy for intimate partner violence: A systematic review and meta-analysis. *Journal of Marital and Family Therapy, 42*(4), 567–583.

Kelly, L., & Westmarland, N. (2015). *Domestic violence perpetrator programmes: Steps towards change.* Project Mirabal Final Report. London and Durham: London Metropolitan University and Durham University.

Lempert, L. (1997). The other side of help: Negative effects in the help-seeking processes of abused women. *Qualitative Sociology, 20*(2), 289–309.

Leone, J. M., Lape, M. E., & Xu, Y. (2014). Women's decisions to not seek formal help for partner violence: A comparison of intimate terrorism and situational couple violence. *Journal of Interpersonal Violence, 29*(10), 1850–1876.

Mendoza, J., & Dolan-Soto, D. R. (2011). Running same-sex batterer groups: Critical reflections on the New York City gay and lesbian anti-violence project and the Toronto David Kelley Services Partner Assault Response Program. In J. L. Ristock (Ed.), *Intimate partner violence in LGBTQ lives* (pp. 274–300). New York and Abingdon: Routledge.

Mitchell, M., Beninger, K., Rahim, N., & Arthur, S. (2013). *Implications of austerity for LGBT people and services.* London: NatCen.

Myhill, A., & Kohl, K. (2016, November 1). The 'Golden Thread': Coercive control and risk assessment for domestic violence. *Journal of Interpersonal Violence.* https://doi.org/10.1177/0886260516675464.

Pence, E. L., & Shephard, M. F. (1999). An introduction: Developing a coordinated community response. In M. F. Shephard & E. L. Pence (Eds.), *Coordinating community responses to domestic violence: Lessons from Duluth and beyond* (pp. 3–25). London: Sage.

Relate. (2016). *All together now: Stronger relationships for a stronger society.* Retrieved September 7, 2019, from https://www.relate.org.uk/sites/default/files/publication-all_together_now-2025_vision_report.pdf

Relate, Relationships Scotland and Marriage Care. (2017). *It takes two: Couple relationships in the UK.* Retrieved August 17, 2019, from https://www.relate.org.uk/sites/default/files/the_way_we_are_now_-_it_takes_two.pdf

Ristock, J. (2002). *No more secrets: Violence in lesbian relationships.* London and New York: Routledge.

Roberts, N. (2018). Inspecting 'transforming rehabilitation': The pitfalls of an austerity managerialist approach to offender supervision. In P. Rushton &

C. Donovan (Eds.), *Austerity policies: Bad ideas in practice* (pp. 121–146). London: Palgrave Macmillan.

Robinson, A. L., Myhill, A., & Wire, J. (2018). Practitioner (mis)understandings of coercive control in England and Wales. *Criminology & Criminal Justice, 18*(1), 29–49.

Roe & Jadoginsky. (n.d.). *Gay, lesbian, bisexual and trans power and control wheel*. Austin, TX: Texas Council on Family Violence. Retrieved September 21, 2019, from http://www.ncdsv.org/images/TCFV_glbt_wheel.pdf

Rollnick, S., Heather, N., Gold, R., & Hall, W. (1992). Development of a short 'readiness to change' questionnaire for use in brief, opportunistic interventions among excessive drinkers. *British Journal of Addiction, 87*(5), 743–754.

Scottish Government & Convention of Scottish Local Authorities (COSLA). (2009). *Safer lives: Changed lives: A shared approach to tackling violence against women in Scotland*. Retrieved September 9, 2019, from https://www.webarchive.org.uk/wayback/archive/20180516085717/http://www.gov.scot/Publications/2009/06/02153519/10

Scottish Government & COSLA. (2018). *Equally safe: Scotland's strategy for preventing and eradicating violence against women and girls*. Retrieved September 9, 2019, from https://www.gov.scot/publications/equally-safe-scotlands-strategy-prevent-eradicate-violence-against-women-girls/

Sharp-Jeffs, N., & Kelly, L. (2016). *Domestic Homicide Review (DHR) case analysis: Report for standing together*. Retrieved August 17, 2019, from http://www.standingtogether.org.uk/news/domestic-homicide-review-case-analysis-report

Simpson, E. K., & Helfrich, C. A. (2014). Oppression and barriers to service for Black, lesbian survivors of intimate partner violence. *Journal of Gay and Lesbian Social Services, 26*(4), 441–465.

Stark, E. (2007). *Coercive control: How men entrap women in personal life*. Oxford: Oxford University Press.

Stonewall. (2018). *LGBT in Britain: Home and communities*. London: Stonewall.

Tavistock Relationships. (2016). *Working relationally with couples where there is situational violence: A policy briefing from Tavistock Relationships*. London: Tavistock Relationships.

Tomsich, E. A., Tunstall, A. M., & Gover, A. R. (2015). Couples counseling and domestic violence. In W. G. Jennings (Ed.), *The Encyclopedia of crime and punishment*. Oxford: Wiley-Blackwell.

Towers, J., & Walby, S. (2012). *Measuring the impact of cuts in public expenditure on the provision of services to prevent violence against women and girls*. Lancaster

University Report for Northern Rock Foundation and Trust for London. Lancaster: Lancaster University.

Trute, B. (1998). Going beyond gender-specific treatments in wife battering: Pro-feminist couple and family therapy. *Aggression & Violent Behavior, 3*(1), 1–15.

Universities UK (UUK). (2016). *Changing the culture: Report of the Universities UK Taskforce examining violence against women, harassment and hate crime affecting university students.* Retrieved May 27, 2017, from https://www.universitiesuk.ac.uk/policy-and-analysis/reports/Documents/2016/changing-the-culture.pdf

Velonis, A. J. (2016). He never did anything you typically think of as abuse: Experiences with violence in controlling and non-controlling relationships in a non-agency sample of women. *Violence Against Women, 22*(9), 1031–1054.

Walby, S., & Towers, J. (2018). Untangling the concept of coercive control: Theorizing domestic violent crime. *Criminology and Criminal Justice, 18*(1), 7–28.

Weeks, J., Heaphy, B., & Donovan, C. (2001). *Same-sex intimacies: Families of choice and other life experiments.* Abingdon: Routledge.

Welsh Government. (2016). *National strategy on violence against women, domestic abuse and sexual violence—2016–2021.* Retrieved September 9, 2019, from https://gweddill.gov.wales/docs/dsjlg/publications/commsafety/161104-national-strategy-en.pdf

6

Conclusion: Telling Different Stories About Intimate Partner Violence and Abuse

Abstract Chapter 6 concludes this book by synthesising our key findings and recapping on how they trouble the existing ways in which intimate partner violence and abuse (IPVA) has been researched and theorised. We highlight the key contributions that we have made, including the importance of recognising identity abuse and experiential power as distinct aspects of LGB and/or T+ people's experiences of domestic violence and abuse (DVA), and conceptualising how victim/survivors' use of physically and non-physically violent resistance as space for reaction can inhibit them from seeing themselves as having been victimised. We argue how the findings from the Coral Project should be translated into a holistic relationship services approach which offers prevention, early intervention and crisis responses. We also identify priorities for the continued research agenda, with a deepening of the understanding of the intersectionality of LGB and/or T+ people's experiences being a key priority. We end by reiterating our hope that our work will not only shape how LGB and/or T+IPVA is understood, researched and responded to, but that our voices from the margins of IPVA scholarship will permeate knowledge production within the mainstream heteronormative, cisnormative IPVA literature too.

© The Author(s) 2020 **161**
C. Donovan, R. Barnes, *Queering Narratives of Domestic Violence and Abuse*, Palgrave Studies in Victims and Victimology, https://doi.org/10.1007/978-3-030-35403-9_6

Keywords Cisnormativity • Coercive control • Domestic violence and abuse • Domestic violence and abuse policy and practice • Intersectionality • Heteronormativity • Intimate partner violence and abuse • Lesbian, gay, bisexual and/or transgender • Mutual abuse • Perpetrators • Power and control • Typologies of domestic violence and abuse • Victims/survivors

6.1   Introduction

This book aimed to queer narratives of intimate partner violence and abuse (IPVA) in LGB and/or T+ people's relationships. We did this by using data from the Coral Project, the first mixed-methods study to focus on LGB and/or T+ people's use of violence and 'abusive' behaviours in their intimate relationships in the UK and, to our knowledge, internationally. In this final chapter, we first outline our key findings and how they trouble existing approaches to knowledge production and theorising within IPVA scholarship. We emphasise how these findings further critical debates in the field and how they should inform future research. The centrality of intersectionality to the future research agenda and the limitations of our own research are also considered. We end with a call for the mainstream IPVA field to embrace the challenges and opportunities which are presented when dominant, heteronormative, cisnormative modes of knowledge production are troubled by stories from the margins.

6.2   Key Findings

The main insights or take-home messages of this book are as follows:

1. Approaching IPVA from a sociological perspective facilitates a broader understanding of how society is implicated in creating the conditions in which IPVA can take place and be supported and colluded with by society's institutions.

    (a) Starting from the public story of domestic violence and abuse (DVA), it becomes clear that patriarchal, heteronormative, cisnormative gender norms shape and influence expectations and sense-making of adult intimate relationships where IPVA is experienced and enacted.

(b) We have argued that the heteronormative, cisnormative gender binary of male/female that is characterised in the public story of DVA is overlaid with a similarly constructed ideal victim/perpetrator binary. This positions the authentic experience of DVA as an extreme type of relationship in which the heterosexual, cisgender (HC) woman is terrorised, blameless and defenceless.

(c) This expanded version of the public story of DVA explains why some of those victimised by DVA do not recognise themselves as victim/survivors because they have utilised space for reaction and fought back against their abusive partner with physical and/or non-physical behaviours.

(d) Our quantitative and qualitative data draw attention to some of the particular ways in which IPVA, power and control operate in LGB and/or T+ people's relationships. Identity abuse and experiential power illustrate how abusive partners can harness cisgendered heteronormativity and homo/bi/transphobia to control, punish and isolate victims/survivors.

2. More nuanced, sociologically informed analyses of quantitative data about IPVA that focus on relationship contexts rather than incidents of behaviour enable different, and more complex, stories to be told with the data.

(a) The gender (a)symmetry debate has profoundly influenced the development of knowledge about IPVA in the relationships of LGB and/or T+ people since they are almost invisible in the population surveys undertaken. Collecting data about the sexuality and gender identity not only of the respondent, but also of their partner, is critical to make sense of indications from large-scale surveys that, proportionately, LGB people report higher rates of IPVA victimisation. Bisexual and trans+ people particularly report high rates in the Coral Project as elsewhere, but trans+ people remain invisible in most general population surveys.

(b) Most IPVA survey instruments fail to capture the relationship context and to measure coercive control (Donovan and Barnes 2019; Myhill and Kelly 2019). This means that LGB and/or T+ people who report enacting physical and non-physical violent resistance behaviours as part of creating space for reaction can be too easily quantitatively categorised as cases of mutual abuse or bidirectional violence.

(c) Reliance on quantitative methods alone results in a very partial, and potentially misleading, story of how IPVA is experienced and/or enacted.

3. Johnson's (2008) typology of IPVA resonates with our quantitative and qualitative data, but echoing other scholars, aspects of this typology and its application require refinement and broadening.

(a) An analysis of survey responses categorising frequencies of using and enacting a range of IPVA behaviours, along with motives for the use of IPVA, points to heterogeneity amongst the groups who report perpetration as well as victimisation. Using Johnson's typology as a guide, we have found evidence of perpetration of coercively controlling violence (CCV) and both physical and non-physical violent resistance (VR) in the high perpetration subgroup; and situational couple physical and non-physical violence (SCV) in the low perpetration subgroup.

(b) In order to more comprehensively examine this heterogeneity, the qualitative data is used to unpack cases that might appear in a survey to be mutual abuse.

(c) Participants' qualitative accounts of 'mutual abuse' destabilise and problematise the public story of DVA's reliance on the female/male, victim/perpetrator binaries.

4. The queering of dominant narratives of IPVA needs to happen within policy and practice too, and responsibility for preventing and responding to IPVA needs to be shared across a wider range of relationships services.

(a) The Coral Project Power, Control and Space for Reaction Wheel is offered as a visual tool to support practitioners' recognition of how partners who are being victimised by CCV may find opportunities to create space for reaction to resist and fight back (physically or non-physically) against the power and control of an abusive partner.

(b) Most survey respondents' behaviours would not reach a threshold of risk that would gain them access to specialist DVA services, including police interest. However, a large minority indicate that they and/or others close to them identify that they have problems with trust, anger and being in control. A similarly large minority indicate that they are ready to make changes in their behaviour in relationships. It is not clear where this apparently highly reflexive sample would be able to access appropriate help. The impact of austerity has led most services to raise their threshold for offering help in order to ration services to those most at risk.

(c) We call for an integrated multi-agency approach to providing relationships services that includes prevention and early intervention as well as crisis intervention, in order to begin to address this unmet need. Prevention should begin with LGB and/or T+-inclusive formal and informal RSE provided in schools, colleges, universities and youth work settings. Early intervention should be available in work settings as well as social services, housing, health and social care settings and relationship counselling services. Crisis interventions should be provided by specialist DVA services and include, and/or have the ability to refer to, carefully designed LGB and/or T+ inclusive perpetrator interventions, for those who require them.

(d) However, relationships services need to be staffed by well-trained and confident practitioners who feel at ease and knowledgeable about the intimate lives of LGB and/or T+ people. This is needed to address the fears that LGB and/or T+ people reported to the Coral Project that they would not be understood by, or would receive discriminatory and/or hostile treatment from, help-providers. Staff also need to be trained to use the Coral Project Power, Control and Space for Reaction Wheel to identify whether, and in what direction, power is operating in the relationships of LGB and/or T+ people who report enacting and/or experiencing IPVA.

(e) The Coral Project findings suggest that LGB and/or T+ people who enact IPVA are most likely to seek individualised help from private, third sector or National Health Service (NHS) counselling/therapeutic services. It is therefore crucial that practitioners within these services are trained not only in the intimate lives of LGB and/or T+ people but also in risk assessment and safety planning.

(f) Practitioners in these and other services need to understand the public story of DVA and how it constrains LGB and/or T+ people from recognising their victimisation, especially when they enact IPVA. They also need to understand, on the one hand, that reliance on a rigid victim/perpetrator binary is overly limited, but on the other, that there is a need to look beyond labels such as 'mutual abuse' or 'bidirectional violence', which neutralise the dynamics of power and control. Thus, assessing the context of someone's intimate relationship is an essential prerequisite to offering appropriate and safe responses, and to knowing when to cross-refer individuals to appropriate specialist DVA services.

6.3   Setting a Research Agenda for Furthering Understanding of IPVA Within LGB and/ or T+ People's Intimate Relationships

The Coral Project was an exploratory mixed-methods research project building on the methodology of the COHSAR project (Donovan and Hester 2014) to explore the use of violent and 'abusive' behaviours in the relationships of LGB and/or T+ people. Our methodology was successful in producing some original and interesting data that sheds light on some important methodological limitations of much research that takes place on IPVA. However, there are also important limitations of our methodology that point to the need for improved methodologies in the future.

1. Quantitative surveys alone can only ever tell a partial story about IPVA but can be enhanced by: collecting data on the sexuality and gender identities of the respondents and the partners they are reporting

on; collecting data on a range of IPVA behaviours but especially including coercively controlling behaviour to establish whether and how power is operating in the relationships; using the measure of 'the last 12 months of your most recent relationship' rather than 'in the last 12 months' in order to have a better sense of what relationships are being reported on; and including questions about motives, impacts and help-seeking. Open-text boxes are useful because they provide opportunities for respondents to explain experiences that they find difficult to fit into the options provided in the survey.

2. Limitations of the Coral Project include having a survey with too many types of IPVA which led to a lot of missing data. Moreover, our decision to use Johnson's typology to guide our analysis was made retrospectively, which meant that we did not incorporate a coercive control measure to the extent that we would have had we designed the survey with this in mind.

3. Whilst the demographics of the survey respondents in terms of 'race' and ethnicity broadly reflect that of the UK population, the numbers were too small to conduct any separate analysis of these and the numbers volunteering to be interviewed were disproportionately small. There was limited opportunity to explore how having a faith or having a physical disability shaped participants' experiences. Further, unlike the survey sample, no one in our interview sample identified as non-binary or genderqueer. Other important aspects of social location, such as having precarious citizenship, were neither reflected in our interview sample nor captured in our survey data.

6.4 The Importance of Intersectionality and Hearing a Wider Range of Stories About LGB and/or T+ People's Experiences of IPVA

Another key priority is to ensure that intersectionality is central to future research about LGB and/or T+ people's intimate relationships.

1. All too commonly, scholars describe LGB and/or T+ people as a homogenous group or inaccurately as a 'community' (see Formby 2017 for a critique of this), and reify sexuality and/or gender identity as the sole explanatory factor in their experiences. In the Coral Project we have striven, both when collecting our data and when analysing and presenting it, to engage with the intersectional dimensions of participants' experiences. That is to say, we have attended to the ways in which participants' multiple identities and social locations (Crenshaw 1991) impact upon their relationship expectations and experiences. This includes the accessibility (perceived or actual) of sources of support, and how others perceive and respond to them. Thus, our participants' experiences were shaped, not only by their sexuality and gender identity but also, by how these intersected with their 'race' or ethnicity, age, faith, disability, socio-economic status, educational attainment and other aspects of their biographies, such as their preference for polyamorous and/or bondage, discipline, sadism and masochism (BDSM) relationships and their geographical location.

2. Yet, as we found, achieving sufficient diversity in samples of LGB and/or T+ people to develop such a comprehensive intersectional analysis is challenging (Hartman 2011; Meezan and Martin 2003). Further, despite our having enlisted the help of over 200 varied social and support groups for LGB and/or T+ people to disseminate our survey, and having used social media to reach LGB and/or T+ people who did not belong to any LGB and/or T+ groups or networks, there were still aspects of homogeneity in the sample—the disproportionate percentage of university-educated participants, for example. Therefore, for us and for future researchers, it is imperative that research design and strategies for recruiting participants are inclusive and proactive in increasing the diversity of samples, such that efforts to tell intersectional stories are rigorous and nuanced, and avoid the risk of being merely tokenistic. Increasing the diversity of research teams is an important aspect of this too: we are very aware that as we are a predominantly white and exclusively cisgender female research team, some prospective participants may not have felt confident that we would be able to understand their lives, and to do so in a non-exploitative, non-oppressive way.

3. Co-producing research with an advisory group yields a wider range of perspectives on research questions, methodologies, language, sampling and recruitment strategies and emerging analyses, and makes researchers more alert to their unconscious assumptions. This was beneficial in the Coral Project, and also provided opportunities for the research findings to be shared with much wider audiences. However, our steering group would have benefited further from the recruitment of a diverse panel of LGB and/or T+ lay people. Yet, any attempts to involve service users must be carefully considered and negotiated so as not to be exploitative or to pay lip service to co-production, and participants should be appropriately remunerated and credited for their contributions (INVOLVE 2019). Piloting research instruments with a diverse pilot sample is also important, in order to test out whether the researchers' terms of reference resonate sufficiently with participants, and to ensure that the language and categories used do not reinforce the othering of those who belong to population(s) that are already marginalised and misunderstood (Carrotte et al. 2016; Westbrook and Saperstein 2015).

6.5   A Final Note: Speaking Back to the Mainstream IPVA Literature

An important point to reiterate in closing is that this is not a book which speaks only to the experiences of LGB and/or T+ people, but one which seeks to trouble and transform some of the key assumptions underpinning knowledge production in the mainstream IPVA field too. Here, what we refer to is research, policy and practice, which—albeit often without making this explicit—restricts its focus to those who are assumed to be both heterosexual and cisgender.

1. From the beginning we made clear our disciplinary roots in sociology and feminist theorising about violence against (HC) women. These roots have led us to argue that, regardless of sexuality or gender identity, patriarchal, heteronormative and cisnormative gendered norms of

intimacy and love shape and inform DVA in adult relationships. The underpinning expectations reflected in the public story of DVA are of unequal overlaying binaries of HC female/male, victim/perpetrator.

2. In order to address the use of violence and 'abusive' behaviours safely and appropriately, practitioners need to recognise that IPVA is enacted for a variety of reasons and with different impacts, and that this is the case regardless of the sexuality and gender identities of each intimate partner.

3. The methodological limitations we identify in the field and in our own work are relevant for all research on IPVA. The population surveys that have included more detail on the gender identity and sexuality of the respondents point to concerning findings on the proportions of LGB people, especially those who are bisexual, reporting IPVA. This suggests that whilst gender is an important lens through which to explore IPVA, it is not the only one. Bringing an intersectional lens to IPVA can only improve knowledge production, both methodologically and theoretically.

4. In addition to making sure that appropriate support and interventions are available, it is also essential that prevention efforts take place both at the individual level and in terms of challenging structural inequalities between and within social groups. Alliances need to be built to embed an intersectional approach that ensures that the work remains political and not individualised, and to transform society rather than simply punish individuals and/or blame victim/survivors. The neoliberal austerity context in UK society forces competition for scarce resources between different groups of victim/survivors and those who enact IPVA (Donovan and Durey 2018) and undermines a coordinated, community response (Pence and Shephard 1999). For the sake of all victim/survivors of DVA, this must be resisted in order to ensure that they all receive the support they need to be safe and expand their space for action. Similarly, work with all perpetrators of DVA must be championed to ensure that they can receive the support and interventions they need to be held accountable and develop non-abusive and non-controlling relationships.

References

Carrotte, E. R., Vella, A. M., Bowring, A. L., Douglas, C., Hellard, M. E., & Lim, M. S. C. (2016). 'I am yet to encounter any survey that actually reflects my life': A qualitative study of inclusivity in sexual health research. *BMC Medical Research Methodology, 16*, 86.

Crenshaw, K. (1991). Mapping the margins: Intersectionality, identity politics, and violence against women of color. *Stanford Law Review, 43*(6), 1241–1299.

Donovan, C., & Barnes, R. (2019, July 26). Re-tangling the concept of coercive control: A view from the margins and a response to Walby and Towers (2018). *Criminology and Criminal Justice*. https://doi.org/10.1177/1748895819864622

Donovan, C., & Durey, M. (2018). 'Well that would be nice, but we can't do that in the current climate': Prioritising services under austerity. In P. Rushton & C. Donovan (Eds.), *Austerity policies: Bad ideas in practice* (pp. 197–220). London: Palgrave Macmillan.

Donovan, C., & Hester, M. (2014). *Domestic violence and sexuality: What's love got to do with it?* Bristol: Policy Press.

Formby, E. (2017). *Exploring LGBT spaces and communities: Contrasting identities, belongings and wellbeing*. Abingdon: Routledge.

Hartman, J. (2011). Finding a needle in a haystack: Methods for sampling in the bisexual community. *Journal of Bisexuality, 11*(1), 64–74.

INVOLVE. (2019). *National standards for public involvement in research*. Southampton: INVOLVE. Retrieved September 27, 2019, from https://www.invo.org.uk/wp-content/uploads/2019/02/71110_A4_Public_Involvement_Standards_v4_WEB.pdf

Johnson, M. P. (2008). *A typology of domestic violence: Intimate terrorism, violent resistance, and situational couple violence*. Boston: Northeastern University Press.

Meezan, J. E., & Martin, J. I. (2003). Exploring current themes in research on gay, lesbian, bisexual and transgender populations. *Journal of Gay & Lesbian Social Services, 15*(1/2), 1–14.

Myhill, A., & Kelly, L. (2019, July 15). Counting with understanding? What is at stake in debates on researching domestic violence. *Criminology & Criminal Justice*. https://doi.org/10.1177/1748895819863098

Pence, E. L., & Shephard, M. F. (1999). An introduction: Developing a coordinated community response. In M. F. Shephard & E. L. Pence (Eds.), *Coordinating community responses to domestic violence: Lessons from Duluth and beyond* (pp. 3–25). London: Sage.

Westbrook, L., & Saperstein, A. (2015). New categories are not enough: Rethinking the measurement of sex and gender in social surveys. *Gender & Society, 29*(4), 534–560.

Appendix A: Combined Abuse Scale Items

Category	Behaviours experienced (64 items)	Behaviours enacted (65 items)
Emotional	Was stopped from seeing/ contacting friends	Stopped partner from seeing/ contacting friends
	Was stopped from seeing/ contacting family	Stopped partner from seeing/ contacting family
	Being regularly insulted or put down	Regularly insulted or put them down
	Accused of not being a real gay man/lesbian	Accused partner of not being a real gay man/lesbian
	Accused of not being a real woman/man	Accused partner of not being a real woman/man
	Threatened with being 'outed'	Threatened to 'out' them
	Told what to do/whom to see	Told them what to do/whom to see
	Wrongly accused of being unfaithful	Accused them of being unfaithful
	Your age used against you	Used their age against them
	Your social class used against you	Used their social class against them
	Your education/intelligence used against you	Used their education/intelligence against them
	Your religion used against you	Used their religion against them
	Your disability used against you	Used their disability against them

(continued)

© The Author(s) 2020
C. Donovan, R. Barnes, *Queering Narratives of Domestic Violence and Abuse*, Palgrave
Studies in Victims and Victimology, https://doi.org/10.1007/978-3-030-35403-9

Category	Behaviours experienced (64 items)	Behaviours enacted (65 items)
	Your race used against you	Used their race against them
	Your sexuality used against you	Used their sexuality against them
	Your gender identity used against you	Used their gender identity against them
	Your property damaged/burnt	Damaged/burnt their property
	Made to do most of the housework	Made them do most of the housework
	Your partner withheld their affection	Withheld affection from them
	Threats to harm someone close to you	Threatened to harm someone close to them
	Threats to kill you	Threatened to kill them
	Malicious/pestering messages (e.g. Facebook, text, phone, email)	Made/sent malicious/pestering messages (e.g. Facebook, text, phone, email)
	Blamed for partner's use of alcohol/drugs	Blamed them for your use of alcohol/drugs
	Blamed for partner's self-harm	Blamed them for your self-harm behaviours
	Partner threatens to commit suicide	Threatened that you would commit suicide
	Being frightened by things your partner says/does	Frightened them with things you said/did
	Had your medicines withheld	Withheld their medicines
	Prevented from attending clinics/ GP appointments	Prevented them from attending clinics/ GP appointments
Financial	You were given pocket money	Gave your partner pocket money
	You were made to account for all your expenditure	Required them to account for all their expenditure
	Partner expected you to go into debt/take out loans/credit to cover their spending	Expected your partner to go into debt/take out loans/credit to cover your spending
	Partner took your cash or used your credit cards/cheques without your permission	Took your partners cash/used their credit cards/cheques without their permission
	Partner regularly expected you to pay most of the joint or relationship expenses	Regularly expected your partner to pay most of the joint or relationship expenses
	Partner blackmailed you for money	Blackmailed your partner for money
	Partner controlled all money coming into the relationship, often spending most of it on themselves	Taken control of all the money coming into the relationship, often spending most of it on yourself

(continued)

Category	Behaviours experienced (64 items)	Behaviours enacted (65 items)
Physical	Being slapped/pushed/shoved	Slapped/pushed/shoved
	Being kicked/punched	Kicked/punched
	Being beaten up	Beaten up
	Being burned	Burned
	Being bitten	Bitten
	Being spat at	Spat at
	Being restrained/held down/tied up	Restrained/held down/tied up
	Being choked/strangled/suffocated	Choked/strangled/suffocated
	Being physically threatened	Physically threatened
	Being forced to take drugs/alcohol	Forced partner to take drugs/alcohol
	Being hit with an object/weapon	Hit with an object/weapon
	Being threatened with an object/weapon	Threatened with an object/weapon
	Being prevented from getting help for injuries	Prevented them from getting help for injuries
	Being stalked/followed by partner	Stalked/followed a partner
	Being locked in house/room by partner	Locked a partner in a house/room
	Your pet(s) abused by partner	Abused a partner's pet(s)
Sexual	Being touched in a way that caused you fear/distress	Touched your partner in a way that caused them fear/distress
	Your partner withheld their affection	Withheld your affection from your partner
	Being ridiculed about your sexual performance	Ridiculed your partner about their sexual performance
	Your partner persuaded or forced you to engage in sexual acts for money/for drugs/for somewhere to stay/or to stay with them	Persuaded or forced your partner to engage in sexual acts for money/drugs/somewhere to stay/or so they could stay with you
	Had private aspects of sexual behaviour made public (including online/mobile phone)	Shared private aspects of your partner's sexual behaviour with other people (incl. online/mobile phone)
	Your partner was unfaithful and boasted about it to you	Been unfaithful and boasted about it to your partner
	Your partner forced you to watch pornography	Forced your partner to watch pornography

(*continued*)

Category	Behaviours experienced (64 items)	Behaviours enacted (65 items)
	Your partner refused your request for safer sex	Refused your partner's request for safer sex
	Your partner did not respect 'safe words' (words used to stop sexual behaviour you are no longer comfortable with—e.g. in BDSM)	Disrespected 'safe' words ('safe words' are words used to stop sexual behaviour you are no longer comfortable with—e.g. in BDSM)
	Being forced into sexual activity (including when under the influence of drugs/alcohol)	Forced partner into sexual activity (incl. while they were under the influence of drugs)
	You had sex for the sake of peace/a quiet life	Had sex with your partner when they were drunk/asleep
	Your partner threatened to sexually assault/abuse you	Used drugs/alcohol to 'spike' your partner's drink
	Your partner raped you	Threatened your partner with sexual assault/abuse
		Raped your partner

Items removed from the final combined scale due to high levels of missing data:

Emotional

- Partner threatened to hurt your children
- Partner actually hurt your children
- Partner threatened to stop your contact with the children
- Partner refused to use the correct pronoun to acknowledge your gender identity
- Had your hormone treatments withheld

Financial

- Partner controlled the money to be used for your transitioning

Appendix B: Table to Accompany the Coral Project Power, Control and Space for Reaction Wheel

© The Author(s) 2020   **177**
C. Donovan, R. Barnes, *Queering Narratives of Domestic Violence and Abuse*, Palgrave
Studies in Victims and Victimology, https://doi.org/10.1007/978-3-030-35403-9

Indicative Behaviours in the Coral Project Power, Control and Space for Reaction Wheel	
Concentric circles	**Explanations**
Relationship rules	In most abusive relationships, regardless of gender or sexuality, two key relationships rules emerge.
	1. The relationship is for the abusive partner and on their terms. This means that they expect to set the terms for the relationship and see it as a vehicle for meeting their own needs. They expect their partner to accept and comply with the terms and are prepared to use a range of abusive behaviours (see the spokes of the Coral Project Power, Control and Space for Reaction Wheel, Chap. 5, p. 145) which both alert their partner to the rules and can be used to punish their partner when they do not comply. Being able to set the terms also means that the abusive partner is able to change their mind, be unpredictable or to state that they do not want to take any responsibility for anything in the relationship (so, e.g. they might not do paid work, they might refuse to take a share of the household duties, childcare or they may explain they have a fear of commitment).
	2. The victim/survivor is responsible for the relationship and for the abusive partner. This means that the victim/survivor is blamed when things go wrong, including when violence/abuse occurs; that they are responsible for 'managing' the abusive partners' relationships with family of origin, friends, including protecting them from others' negative criticism about their behaviour; provide support and care for the abusive partner when they are upset by the outside world, their employer, their difficulties coping with life, and even after they have been violent and/or abusive. Because the victim/survivor is held responsible for the relationship, abusive partners are often extremely reluctant to let go and employ different ways of persuading victim/survivors to stay or return to the abusive relationship or to punish them for leaving/staying away. Conversely, it is also the case that victim/survivors might experience themselves as emotionally 'stronger' than their abusive partner and often believe that they should take care of them (see practices of love).
Power and control	The range of behaviours that are employed by abusive partners are all intended to exert power and control over the victim/survivor so that the relationship rules are understood and complied with; including punishment for breaking the rules.

(continued)

Indicative Behaviours in the Coral Project Power, Control and Space for Reaction Wheel	
Concentric circles	Explanations
Practices of love	Abusive partners might engage in many practices of love which act to confuse the victim/survivor about what is happening in the relationship, how to understand it and how to recognise and name their experience as DVA. Many abusive relationships are not experienced negatively all of the time. Very often abusive relationships can have 'happy' periods or times when victim/survivors feel they are loved and needed by an abusive partner. In this way expressions of love can in themselves form part of the violence/abuse as they confuse, manipulate and act to glue victim/survivors into abusive relationships. 1. *Declarations of love*: abusive partners might declare their love for a partner especially when their partner is thinking about/threatening to and/or actually leaving. This kind of declaration is often accompanied by; 2. *Expressions of need/neediness*: abusive partners talk about why they behave the way they do in an effort to elicit forgiveness, care and support and love from their partner; and to persuade them to stay in the abusive relationship. These revelations often lead to: 3. *Expectations of care*: abusive partners often elicit feelings in victim/survivors that obligate them to respond to the declarations of love and expressions of need/neediness their abusive partners reveal. This compounds their sense that they are responsible for looking after their abusive partner and that they are the emotionally 'stronger' partner who should protect and remain loyal to their partner.

(*continued*)

Indicative Behaviours in the Coral Project Power, Control and Space for Reaction Wheel	
Concentric circles	Explanations
Intersecting identities	Abusive partners and victim/survivors rarely identify in simple ways. Most experience their world in ways that are shaped by how their identity is assumed to be by those around them in their family/friendship networks as well as by professionals in more formal contexts; and by how they identify themselves. This can include their sexuality, 'race' and/or ethnicity, their age, their social class, their gender, their faith and whether they are able-bodied or not. When working with abusive partners, being aware of what intersecting identities they inhabit will help understand: 1. how they perceive their behaviours, including their moral code and/or whether they normalise their behaviours. This will also impact on how they make sense of how their partner might be experiencing their abusive behaviour 2. their likely support networks and whether these might reinforce abusive relationships or support non-abusive relationships 3. their willingness to acknowledge their abusive behaviours and to change When working with those victimised, being aware of what intersecting identities they inhabit will help understand: 1. how they perceive their experiences, including their moral code and/or whether they normalise what is happening. This will also impact on how they make sense of their abusive partners' behaviours. 2. their likely support networks and whether these might reinforce abusive relationships or support non-abusive relationships 3. their perception of how they might seek help and who they might seek help from, including reporting to the police.

Indicative behaviours for spokes in the Coral Project Power, Control and Space for Reaction Wheel	
Spokes in the Wheel	Indicative examples
Coercion and threats	Making and/or carrying out threats to hurt a partner; threatening to leave them and/or to commit suicide, driving recklessly to frighten them, making them drop charges, making them do illegal things, convincing them that the police or other help-providers will be discriminatory and/or hostile to them and/or to the abusive partner.
Intimidation	Making a partner afraid with looks, actions, gestures, weapons; destroying their property/things; abusing pets.
Emotional abuse	Putting a partner down; making them feel bad about themselves; calling them names; making them think they're crazy; playing mind games; humiliating them; making them feel guilty; undermining their sense of self so that they believes that they are incompetent, stupid, 'wrong', to blame; claiming that nobody will take them seriously if they speak to anybody; making them believe they are lucky to be in a relationship with them.
Using isolation	Controlling what a partner does, who they see and/or talk to, what they read or watch on the television and/or computer and/or social media and where they go; limiting their contacts with the outside world; using jealousy to justify their own actions.
Minimising, denying and blaming	Making light of the abuse and not taking concerns about it seriously; saying the abuse didn't happen, shifting the responsibility for the abuse onto a partner, other external factors, or on their own problems (substance use, unhappy, abusive childhoods etc.)
Using children	Making a partner feel guilty about their children; undermining their parenting; using the children to relay messages; using visitation to harass them; threatening to take children away; telling lies to the children about them.
Economic abuse	Preventing a partner from getting or keeping a job; expecting to be paid for, bills be paid, be given expensive gifts to be financially subsidised; making them ask for money; giving them an allowance; taking their money; not letting them know about/have access to the household income; running up debts without their knowledge (e.g. by not paying bills, taking out loans); making all big decisions about how money will be spent.

(continued)

Indicative behaviours for spokes in the Coral Project Power, Control and Space for Reaction Wheel

Spokes in the Wheel	Indicative examples
Physical abuse	Slapping/pushing/shoving; physically threatening a partner; kicking/punching; restraining/holding them down/tying them up; stalking/following them; beating up; choking/strangling/ suffocating; locking them out of the house/room; hitting them with an object/weapon; biting; abducting them and keeping them somewhere against their will.
Sexual abuse	Pressuring a partner to have sex for sake of peace or to 'make-up'; rejecting a partner sexually and only having sex on their terms; touching a partner in ways that causes fear/ alarm/distress; forcing into sexual activity, including rape, forcing them to watch or enact pornography; hurting during sex; disrespecting 'safe' words/boundaries; sexually assaulting/abusing; refusing requests for safer sex.
Entitlement abuse	Treating a partner like a servant; making all the big decisions; being the one to define roles in the relationship (of women and men; or how partners in same-sex relationships should act); assuming that their social identities give them higher social status in the relationship and treating their partner as if they are less worthy of respect and so on; using faith, 'race', social class, education as a justification for inequalities in the relationship; claiming that their behaviour is normal and that 'everyone else' would agree.
Identity abuse	Threatening to out or actually outing their partner's sexuality, gender (or birth gender) identity or HIV status to their employer/colleagues, Faith community, family of origin, children's services; exerting experiential power by assuming that their longer experience of being out means they have better authority about what it is to be authentically LGB and/ or T+; undermining a partner's sense of self as a women, man, lesbian, gay man, bisexual women or man, a trans women or man or a non-binary gendered or gender queer person; controlling what they look like, what clothes they wear, what hair style they have, their 'look' and behaviours; threatening to or withdrawing their medication, hormones, physical care supports; refusing them financial support for the costs of their gender transition and/or medication.

(continued)

Indicative behaviours for spokes in the Coral Project Power, Control and Space for Reaction Wheel	
Spokes in the Wheel	Indicative examples
Space for reaction	Fighting back in self-defensive and/or retaliatory ways against an abusive partner with physical and non-physical violence: arguing, shouting, screaming back; becoming angry, refusing to conform to an abusive partner's demands, for example, in relation to wearing particular clothes and make-up. Fighting back is not only understood as incident-based but might become the relationship demeanour of the victim/survivor and resistance might become enacted in an ongoing way for the duration of the relationship. This might include planning in advance when and how a relationship might be left. While space for reaction reflects the agency and resistance of victim/survivors the concentric circles of relationship rules, power and control, intersecting identities and practices of love are still in play. Victim/survivors may believe they are striving to regain some equality in the relationship and fail to recognise their victimisation because of their own use of IPVA and/or because they do not recognise themselves in the ideal, defenceless, blameless victim. Importantly, space for reaction may not necessarily be successful, and may be very costly in a range of ways. This spoke breaks the outer rim of the wheel to indicate that the power and control of the abusive partner, as represented by the wheel, can be broken. Help-seeking can help to break the circle. Help-seeking is not straightforward and can involve approaching both informal and formal sources of help over time.

This table was originally published in Catherine Donovan and Marianne Hester, *Domestic Violence and Sexuality: What's Love Got to Do with It?* (pp. 208–209). Republished with permission of Policy Press (an imprint of Bristol University Press, UK). Updated to reflect the findings from the Coral Project.

Index[1]

---

[1] Note: Page numbers followed by 'n' refer to notes.

© The Author(s) 2020   **185**
C. Donovan, R. Barnes, *Queering Narratives of Domestic Violence and Abuse*, Palgrave
Studies in Victims and Victimology, https://doi.org/10.1007/978-3-030-35403-9

CPI Antony Rowe
Eastbourne, UK
February 17, 2020